How to Do Good After Prison

A Handbook for Successful Reentry

Michael B. Jackson

> *"I know the plans I have for you, declared the Lord, plans to prosper you and not to harm you, plan to give you hope and a future".*
>
> *– (Jeremiah 20:11)*

In Loving Memory of my son
Kevin Lamont Jackson
May 10, 1970 – July 28, 2001

Library of Congress Control Number: 2001116657
ISBN: 9 780970 743602

Joint FX Press
PMB #104, 621 Beverly/Rancocas Rd.
Willingboro, NJ 08046
609-877-8071
609-877-8071 fax
press@jointfx.com
www.jointfx.com

"Mr. Jackson, you have been arrested 9 times and convicted 8 times. You have violated parole 5 times and you violated probation 2 times. What do you have to say for yourself?"
"Uhh, My Bad?"
The Judge

About the Author

Raised in a Newark, New Jersey housing project, Michael B. Jackson was introduced to a life of crime and heroin addiction at an early age. At 18, he made his first  trip to prison, and for the next ten years was in an out of prison for parole violations and new offenses. Like so many inmates, he became more comfortable behind bars than in the outside world.

One day Jackson finally "got it" and made a commitment to change his life for the better. Channeling his anger and resentment for positive purposes, he began to put back the pieces of his self-esteem and character. In 1979, after spending several months in a halfway house, he was paroled and has never returned to prison. Within ten months of his release, Jackson gained custody of his son who at eight years of age had become involved in petty crimes.

Today, Jackson is an author, motivational speaker, businessman and the founder of www.Jointfx.com – a website devoted to helping formerly incarcerated people and their families find success during and after prison. He also founded and hosts the online radio talk program, "Prison Nation Radio w/ Michael B. Jackson". Employed by a state corrections agency for 23 years, Jackson conducts seminars and training sessions on topics related to prisoner reentry success after prison. He has appeared on many radio and TV shows.

INTRODUCTION

Doing What You Got to Do!

One icy cold day in January, a while back, I was waiting in a long line at the carwash with many other people trying to get the dirt and road salt off our rides after a recent snowstorm. The line was moving very slowly and when I finally got closer to the entrance, I could see why. There was only one black dude, about sixty, working the entrance. As well as being cold as hell that day, it was windy and with that water spraying around didn't help. I wondered how he stayed out there all alone in the freezing weather to work at that car wash that day. The dude had to be cold and tired but went about his job like a hero. He handed each customer his or her ticket, vacuumed each car, steamed all four tires & rims, hit the hard-to-reach places with a long-handled brush, and then he hooked the tow chain under the front of the car and moved on to the next one, all the time being cordial and friendly toward each customer. I overheard a woman ask him how he could stand it out there and without breaking stride he said, "I'm just doing what I got to do, ma'am"

Just doing what I got to do. Those words stuck with me because so many times when asked why he did what he did to get locked up a guy will say, "I did what I had to do" – or words to that effect. As if selling drugs, or sticking up that store, or doing whatever he did to get busted again was his only option in life. Usually, "I did what I had to do" really means, "I did what I wanted to do".

While sitting there in my ride with the heat turned up high and the music even higher, I thought to myself, there was a man doing what he had to do to get where he wanted to be. I even had to question whether I would be able to do what he was doing, to make a living.

Would I have the guts to stand out there in freezing weather all day for the minimal pay the car wash offers? I tried to think of periods over the past twenty years when I could truly say I paid the price and overcame difficult times and circumstances in order to be successful.

My first job at the fiberglass-recycling factory in the winter of 1979 immediately came to mind. That had to be the worst job ever. Every day I would leave that factory in pain with millions of tiny sharp needle-like shards of fiberglass sticking in my clothing and skin. I would stand up on the bus ride home even though there were plenty of empty seats because sitting down would drive the needles deeper into my skin and hurt like hell. I would sit in the bathtub for hours when I got home to try and soak the glass out of my skin. It did not work.

I could hardly get up at five every morning, six days a week, to get to that factory by six-thirty, but I did it every day because I knew that it was better than being in prison. At the end of my shift, I could go home and be a free man.

In the past, I would have never stayed with a job like that, or any job, for that matter. That is probably why I had been sent back for three (3) new commitments and five (5) parole violations over a ten-year (10) span, back in the day.

The job was awful but it was different that time. I was different also. I was committed to making my jail break permanent. I was never going back to prison and I knew that I had to pay my dues. I looked at that job as just one of the tests I was going to have to pass in order to move on to better things. It was tough and I could not see myself working there for long periods of time. I kept my focus on a better future. I was fortunate enough to find a better job after a few months. It still was not where I wanted to be, but it was a more desirable and higher paying job and that was a step up and forward. I also worked over-time and part-time jobs, until I finally got to where I wanted to be.

How many men today can honestly say that they would be willing to work at the car wash, or the fiberglass factory in 30-degree weather, if that was all that was available in the beginning? Sure, most men in prison will make all kinds of promises about what they're going to do to succeed after prison, but how many are truly prepared to do what you have to do?

According to the U.S. Bureau of Prisons (2004), two-thirds (approx. 415,000) of the 650,000 people released from prison each year will return to prison within twelve to thirty-six months of release for parole violations or new offenses. The cost of maintaining the more than two million people crowded into the prisons in this country has become too much of a financial burden, so many States are attempting to address some of the so-called "barriers" against the successful re-entry of prisoners back into society with policy changes and other programs and services.

There is a very good chance that despite their best efforts, the prison system will never be equipped to properly prepare prisoners to re-enter and succeed in society. Even with the best programs and services, public attitudes toward convicted felons cannot be legislated. Under any circumstances, it took a long time for things to get the way they are and it is not likely to change overnight, if ever.

Unfortunately, regardless of the best efforts of anyone, there will always be men who will return to prison over and over again because there will always be the so-called "barriers" that contribute to the high failure rate for people returning after release from prison. The long list of complex and systemic "barriers" includes negative public policies and opinions towards convicted-felons; a lack of programs and resources for newly incarcerated and formerly incarcerated people; mental/physical health issues; and the fact that most people released from prison are just not prepared to return to society.

Then there is that self-inflicted "barrier," a bad attitude or wrong attitude that keeps so many people going back. The men and women who intend to keep doing what they have been doing because they do not mind doing the time. They have become what I call prisonized, and lockdown is a comfort zone for them. For some, being out of prison can be like a fish out of water. They cannot make it on the outside, or they do not believe that they can make it, so they just flop around until they are dead or wind up back in prison.

Yet, I believe the majority of those 433,000 people returning to prison every year want to be successful and not go back. They would rather be on the street working and supporting a family, instead of taking from them. More formerly incarcerated people would be successful after prison, if they knew how to do it.

Too many men create their own, or "self-inflict", barriers and perpetuate their own ultimate downfall because of an overall lack of knowledge, preparation, and commitment.

Unfortunately, a man involved in the criminal justice system today, who is looking to change his life for the better, cannot wait for possible reforms promising programs, services, resources, and support. He has bills to pay now. Somewhere along the lines every man must be responsible for his own success and find a way to succeed.

This book is intended to inspire, motivate, encourage, and enlighten the man committed to his own success after prison; it is intended to help this individual organize and prepare himself to recognize, understand, and overcome the barriers he will experience as a formerly incarcerated person trying to make it in society.

This book represents my personal and professional experiences and observations, first from early on in my life while formerly incarcerated, and then as a professional the past twenty years working in private and government prisons and post-release corrections. I have also borrowed from the wisdom of other formerly incarcerated people who have broken the cycle and made it. I have also learned from those who have not.

Of course, reading this book will not guarantee anyone success after prison and it probably will not be the cause of mass layoffs of corrections officers across the country. There are no magic potions of advice or "shortcuts to success. Achieving success and living tho so-called "straight life" – after years in the underside – it is hard work but it can be done.

Will there ever be the moment when each person coming out of prison has gone on to live a successful straight life, never returning to prison or a life of crime again? The day when all the empty prisons have been converted to warehouses, malls, or condominiums because all the bad guys have gone straight. Will there ever be the day when every man paroled or released from prison will have learned his lesson and go on to become a responsible father to his children, a dependable and supportive, companion/lover to one's women, and an overall positive member of the community, one whose mother would be proud? Would there ever be a day when everyone was actually doing what he had to do? Probably not. However, I believe more people want to do better, and I believe more people would actually do better if they were better prepared and committed to doing whatever it takes to never return to prison again. When things are at their worst, it is easy for some to give up and go negative. I challenge each man who says he wants to change to fight the urge to seek refuge in the prison and to take responsibility for one's own successes and failures. Never... Ever... give up! Have faith in GOD and have confidence in yourself. Continue to do the right things and good things will happen for you. It is up to you to make it happen for yourself – or not.

Jailin Too Long

"I told you a thousand times, turn your cellphone off if you have to hide under the bed.

"For me there is a time ... when we have to turn the mirror around, because for me it is almost analgesic to talk about what the white man is doing against us. And it keeps a person frozen in their seat; it keeps you frozen in your hole you're sitting in." - Bill Cosby

PART ONE

Doing Time in Prison

In the seventies and early eighties, when I was deep into my run, it was all about a kinder and gentler prison system that focused on "rehabilitation". It was during that era when "convicts" became "inmates" or "residents"; when "guards" became "correctional officers" and "prisons" became "correctional centers".

Lockups became a place where some guys, such as me, would go to chill when things got too complicated out on the streets. It was a place where you would mingle and socialize with people that you had not seen in a while. Dope fiends, such as myself, could clean up their bodies, minds, and souls by running laps around the yard, pumping iron, and doing 500-1000 push-ups every day to get in peak shape. A man could go into prison a school dropout and leave a few years later with a college degree. The three guaranteed meals a day, hot showers, and clean linen twice a week were like icing on the cake. "Jailing" had become something of an art form or a sport and the guys caught up in the revolving door were all talented and intelligent. Some guys, like me, for instance, were so good at "jailing" that we could not stop.

In the seventies and eighties there was also a lot of emphasis on government/prison sponsored educational, vocational and skills training programs and on counseling services in the prisons for inmates.

> All the educational and training programs in the world are no guarantees or a barometer in predicting a person's chances of success or failure after prison. Ask all those men and women who had earned college degrees while in prison – only to be revoked for a dumb parole

> violation such as smoking a joint the day before
> a drug test, or blowing off reporting because of
> being too lazy to get out of bed.

When things get rough, common sense, good decision-making and self-motivation will do more than a college degree every time. Without these three things you are in trouble!

Lately, more corrections departments are realizing the importance of better preparing an inmate for successful employment after they leave prison. There are many government-sponsored inmate training and post-release programs being implemented these days.

The state of New Jersey has just announced the "Strategy for Safe Streets and Neighborhoods" The strategy is said to address issues of enforcement, prevention and re-entry with an emphasis on reducing gang violence, violent crime and recidivism. The "reentry" component of the plan is of particular interest because, if it goes the way it is intended, it should provide many opportunities for formerly incarcerated people, their families and the community. It is almost like the good old days – "REHABILTATION" reincarnated.

The problem is that, just like back in the day, too many of the men and women in prison do not take advantage of what is available to them. If you are unfortunate enough to be in prison, yet fortunate enough to be in a prison where there are courses, training, programs and self-improvement programs you should take maximum advantage of these opportunities.

Even with programs to assist there will be plenty of gaps that each person will have to fill for him or herself. The real and meaningful progress in self-improvement has to be done independently. Each person will have to become self-motivated and self-committed to doing whatever it takes to ensure that when leaving the prison that individual is a better, more capable person than they were when he or she came in. No excuse is acceptable. Do something!

Many of the men and women in prison are not first-timers. Many are among the two-thirds of released inmates who return to prison within a year or so for new offenses or parole violations, which I mentioned earlier. Despite all of the bitching and moaning that he does about how rough it is in there, each man must first realize how comfortable and content he actually is in prison. Anyone leaving prison can be successful and make a new life for him or herself and achieve their piece of the American dream. If you are in doing time and you think you want to pull it together this time, do not take it lightly. Start right away.

> Take advantage of a bad situation and use the time in lockdown to better yourself in some way. Do not waste your time!

Here are some suggestions that may help organize prison time in a way that can aid in preparing one to be successful after prison

Recognize & Accept a Higher Power

> An awareness of your spirituality will help bring you the awareness, ability, and strength to create a better life for yourself and others.

When I say "Higher Power," I'm not talking about the ripped weight-lifting guy who sleeps in the bunk above you. I'm talking about a Spiritually Higher Power. Most guys in prison should count their blessings because despite outward appearances they have a lot to be thankful for. The mere fact that some guys are even alive today – considering their past behavior – should be enough to have some dudes on their knees praying three times a day. Men with a possibility of gaining parole or release one day should be especially thankful. Recognizing a Higher Power, outside yourself, will help you discover the higher power within yourself.

> *"Failing to Prepare is preparing to fail"*
> –Bill Walton (Hall of Fame Basketball Player)

Be Accountable/Responsible

Acknowledge and accept responsibility for the things you have done in the past and for the things you will do in the future

Accountability is very important to a person's quest to live right and live well after prison. No one can go around doing what he or she wants to do without eventually having to answer to someone for it. So far, most men in prison have only been accountable to the prison system. Acknowledge and accept responsibility for the things you have done and the things you will do in the future. Acknowledge and accept responsibility for who you have been, for who you are, and for who you intend to be. Placing blame outside you will only provide a convenient excuse to quit when things get tough. Do not harbor hate and resentment, especially over things and people you cannot change or control. The stress will kill you.

Respect the Authority

Whatever the case, men in prison cannot afford to be caught up in feuds and altercations with prison personnel, because it is obvious who has more to lose – and it is not them.

Can you imagine the day when all prison correctional officers approach and perform their job in a mature, intelligent, respectful and responsible manner and represent the uniform with honor and integrity? Prison would be sweet if they would just get rid of all the COs? Sure, I realize that concept is even crazier than the idea of every crook going straight. Just like incarcerated people, prison officers and parole officers come in all flavors. Most are decent people who find that they can do their jobs without trying to be hard. Whatever the case, men in prison cannot afford to be caught up in feuds and altercations with prison personnel, because it is obvious who has more to lose – and it is not them. Respect the authority, even if you do not respect the person it is attached to. Avoiding and/or dealing with a guard who is on your case is much more difficult that getting around a conflict with another person. That is mainly because of the natural power and influence the guards have over inmates. It may be difficult to avoid problems altogether, but stay focused on your own future and let the simple stuff go. Rise above and move beyond.

Commit to Your Own Success

> The successful man has to be committed to himself first.

Make a commitment to yourself to live your life with honor, success, integrity, responsibility, and respectability in everything you do beginning now. Commit to do well and to live your life in a positive and peaceful manner. Commit to yourself first before you even think about making any commitments to others. The successful man has to want to do it for himself.

Let it Go: Forgive Yourself

> Believe that you are a better person than you appear to be in that prison uniform and commit to do better.

Even the most successful person must never forget or take for granted the harm and pain that he may have caused others in the past. By the same token, it is important that you make peace and forgive yourself for your past errors in judgment and behavior. Believe that you are a better person than you appear to be in that prison clothing and commit to do better.

Choose Your World

Stick with people who have the same sincere commitments as you do to get out and stay out of prison. Set your priorities and create the world you want around you.

The people you hang around with in the prison will say a lot about who you are and also who – and what – you intend to be in the future. If you are hanging out with the wrong crowd in the joint, you are going to have problems. Place yourself around people who are positive-minded and not caught up in all of the jailhouse drama. Stick with people who have the same sincere commitments as you do to get out and stay out of prison. Set your priorities and create the world you want around you.

Education & Training

How well you prepare yourself while still inside will go a long way toward determining whether you will still be on the street and doing well a year after parole. Or whether you will be back in lockdown trying to justify your failure and convince everyone that it is not your fault.

Along with commitment, attitude, good decision-making, heart, and a few breaks here and there, education is very important in the success of some coming out of prison. How well you prepare yourself while still inside will go a long way toward determining whether you will still be on the street and doing well a year after parole. Or whether you will be back in the lockdown justifying your failure and trying to convince everyone that it is not your fault.

There is a very high rate of illiteracy among prison inmates. If your reading level is low, try to get tutoring... There is a very high rate of illiteracy among prison inmates. If your reading level is low, try to get tutoring... To be successful you must put aside foolish pride and ask for help where you need it. The world is into the age of technology. Get books and magazines on computers and the Internet, or World Wide Web (www). The Internet opens up a world of resources, opportunities, and information. In addition, many jobs call for you to use a computer, in some form or fashion. If you do not have a computer at home, check with the public libraries in your area. Sometimes the library offers access to Internet connected computers and you can use these to search for a job, and other things. Being aware of the Internet and how it works will definitely give you an edge.

> There is a very high rate of illiteracy among prison inmates. If your reading level is low, try to get tutoring... To be successful you must put aside foolish pride and ask for help where you need it.

If possible, work towards your GED and take college courses and vocational training. Take advantage of all opportunities that will help prepare you for a new life in a New World. Spend time in the prison library, if there is one. If there is no library, or when you have exhausted and progressed beyond the resources available inside the prison, seek more knowledge from outside through mail order sources. Have your family send you books and other self-improvement tools.

Work on your writing, spelling and penmanship skills. There are few things more detrimental to your chances of getting a job than turning in a job application that is sloppy and full of misspelled words. Keeping a personal journal is a good habit to develop. Write something in it every day, even if only a few sentences.

Get Your Papers in Order

While many people lose these documents when they are incarcerated, you can begin to collect them again from the prison, by mail or with the help of someone on the outside.

In order to get a job, apply for public benefits (such as general assistance, food stamps or Medicaid) or other programs, get job training, counseling, open a bank account or even apply for an apartment, you will need to have as many identification documents in hand as possible. Some possible forms of I.D. are: driver's license, passport, marriage or divorce record, adoption record, military record, school I.D., A certification from the prison with photo, name, age, date of birth and parent's name should also be sufficient. Probably the most important documents are birth certificates, social security cards and driver's licenses. While many people lose these documents when they are incarcerated, you can begin to collect them again from the prison, by mail or with the help of someone on the outside. Having proper ID is extremely important and you should begin gathering as much as you can as soon as possible.

(See Appendix A for the Employment Information Handbook; a complete address guide to assist you in obtaining your vital papers preparing for, getting and maintaining a job and other useful information)

Read to Achieve & to Grow

Read books, magazines, newspapers, the prison handbook, comic books, cereal boxes, self-improvement books and vocabulary builders, whatever!

Reading is the best way to accomplish these goals. Read books, magazines, newspapers, the prison handbook, comic books, cereal boxes, "self-improvement" books and vocabulary builders. Read a variety of literature styles and subject topics. It is good to broaden your horizons and important to learn about the broader world.

Recommended Reading

Bible and/or Qur'an

How to Love & Inspire Your Man After Prison
Michael B. Jackson

Como Cumplir Con Tus Obligaciones Al Salir De La Prision: Guia practica para una vida mejor
Michael B. Jackson

How to Love & Inspire Your Man After Prison
Michael B. Jackson

The Seven Habits of Highly Successful People
Stephen R. Covey

Long Walk to Freedom
Nelson Mandela

Rich Dad, Poor Dad
Robert T. Kiyosaki

Manchild in the Promise Land
Claude Brown

Rock This
Chris Rock

Attitude is Everything
Keith Harrell

Playboy, Hustler, Black Tail Magazine, Comic Books, The Parole Manual...

Whatever you do, just read!

Learn to Speak Intelligently

> You do not have to try and come off like Barack Obama, but, you want to get ahead you have to be able to carry on a conversation that does not include any reference to prison, drugs, crime, your sexual prowess or other street topics.

You do not have to try and come off like Barack Obama, but, you want to get ahead you have to be able to carry on a conversation that does not include any reference to prison, drugs, crime, your sexual prowess or other street topics. Spend time working on your speaking and conversational skills. Strengthen your personal vocabulary and your knowledge and use of proper grammar. The manner in which you speak may be as important as that of which you speak. When you begin to meet new people who are not familiar with the prison culture, you will want to be able to hold an intelligent conversation without embarrassing yourself and the person you are talking to. The slick jailhouse banter will fly in the real world. Once again, reading is the best and most interesting way to broaden the scope of your worldly knowledge. Reading also helps to overcome the sensory deprivation effects the prison environment can have on you. Reading can take your mind outside the prison walls so that you can stay in touch with the real world. Becoming a good listener and observer are two qualities that make for a wiser, more aware person.

Be Positive & Confident

> Be confident, but not arrogant or obnoxious...

Stay Committed! Never doubt yourself and never let anyone dissuade you from following your instincts that tell you what is, and is not, good for you. Be confident, but not arrogant or obnoxious. Be assertive, but not aggressive. Be stubborn and strong, yet not so strong that you cannot adjust and adapt to the normal changes in life and to the rights and needs of others.

Be Proactive in Your Own Success

Do not spend time focusing on what the prison does not do for you. You have to be self-motivated and self-inspired and do for yourself.

You cannot wait for the Prison to give you anything except a hard time. Do not spend time focusing on what the prison does not do for you. You have to be self-motivated and self-inspired and do for yourself. You have to be self-motivated and self-inspired and do it for yourself. Inmates should form their own support groups with other men who may want to get out and stay out, just as you do. People in prison and those on the outside can help one another by sharing positive support and encouragement. You want to associate with people who share a mutual respect and trust for one another.

Invite people from the outside, as well as various prison staff to speak to your group about the things that will help you in the real world. More people than you might expect would be willing to come in and talk to a group of inmates who are trying to better themselves.

Practice Social & Life Skills

Learn and understand personal banking, opening accounts, filling out checks, check clearance procedures, penalty costs, etc.

Learn and understand how the real world works and what you need to do to get along in it. Learn how to budget and get the most out of your money. This is important no matter how much money you earn. Learn and understand personal banking, opening accounts, filling out checks, check clearance procedures, penalty costs, etc. You will never be completely accepted in the "real world" until you have a legitimate bank checking and savings account. A driver's license, social security card, and birth certificate are also very important documents that everyone should have.

As mentioned earlier, it is a good idea to attempt to obtain a copy of your birth certificate while still inside. Sometimes it is possible to get duplicate copies through the mail, from the records department in the city of your birth.

(See Appendix A for addresses to getting your documents)

Develop Good Work Habits

> The important thing is that you find a way to put pride into your work, whatever it is. Build a work ethic and experience people being dependent on you and the job that you do.

If you are in prison and you do not already have a job, get one! Try to get a job that requires thought and skills, such as in an office or the library. It would be ideal if an inmate could get a job that would prepare him for a real job on the street, but that is not always possible. Do not worry about that. The important thing is that you find a way to put pride into your work, whatever it is. Build a work ethic and experience people being dependent on you and the job that you do.

> Develop good work habits such as getting up
> early on your own and being on time.

If possible, get an alarm clock and do not wait for the guard to wake you up every morning. Learn to follow instructions, how to work on your own, and how to make decisions. To develop punctuality and self-discipline, it is good to practice setting and following a daily schedule.

Practice Goal Setting

> Stretch yourself by reaching higher to maximize
> your potential.

Short and long term goals are very important in the life of a successful man after prison. Do not try to make up for the years you wasted in prison and running the streets. Set short-term goals for yourself. Acknowledge each time you reach a goal and reward yourself. Set time frames and work your way up to where you want to be in your new life. Take it slow and steady. You have the rest of your life ahead of you.

When it seems you have reached your goals, do not settle and get complacent. In other words, do not be happy just to be in the game. Stretch yourself by reaching higher to maximize your potential. Should you fail occasionally, so what. It does not mean that you are automatically a failure and on your way back to prison. Just keep going and keep it legitimate.

> One of the first goals you might want to
> consider setting for yourself is to successfully
> complete parole.
>
> Remember your first goal is to stay out of
> prison.

Never forget!

Develop Your Employability Level

Lack of employment is a major contributor in
the failure and return to prison of most people.

Lack of employment is a major contributor in the failure and return to prison of most people. Finding a job is also one of the most difficult challenges most formerly incarcerated people will face. It is not just getting a job, but getting a job that pays a decent wage to live on and possibly even support a family. An attractive resume package is needed to present to employers to overcome the former incarceration factor. It can be tricky and frustrating, but it can be done.

Learn job search skills such as filling out job applications. Start to put together a resume. Try to get copies of different job applications and practice filling them out. It does not matter what employer the applications are geared for. The point is for you to become familiar with the language and content on job applications and with how you will answer the questions.

Each person must decide how much information
he is going to divulge about his past.

Virtually all job applications ask the applicant whether they have ever been convicted of a crime. Men coming out of prison must adjust to their own unique situation. Each person must decide how much information he is going to divulge about his past. You will have to make a call based on how you think your honesty will affect your chances of being considered for the job. It also gets sticky trying to fill the gaps in time when trying to explain your whereabouts for the past several years and the fact that you had no job. You may have to be creative. If you can be honest and work through it, fine. Not all situations will let you do that. You also may be able to use your work assignments and training from inside as work experience. Sometimes employers check past employers and references and sometimes they do not.

> Endorsements are sacred and hard to come by. Once someone has backed you, you have an obligation to respect and to represent those people with dignity.

It could be beneficial if you could get references from staff or volunteers you meet in the prison, like the chaplain, a teacher, a social worker or your work detail supervisor. Even a reference from a guard could go a long way. Maybe you have made acquaintances through the mail or come into contact with people who would be good references. If you are lucky enough to get people to agree to stand for you or to sponsor you, understand that references are sacred and that you must treat them as such. Once a person has backed you, they put their personal reputation and credibility on the line. You have an obligation to respect and to represent your supporters and sponsors well. You probably will only get one chance to betray the trust that others put in you.

(See Appendix A for the Employment Information Handbook; a complete guide to assist you in preparing for, getting and maintaining a job and other useful information)

Prepare to Sell Yourself

> You will need to make the employer understand that he/she will never regret giving you a

chance to prove yourself

Remember, when going after a job do not be timid. You must sell yourself like you are a hot product. Be assertive, but realistic. There are many occupations where your background will not get in the way. You will need to make the employer understand that he/she will never regret giving you a chance to prove yourself. There are many businesses looking for responsible and competent people to work for them. You just have to keep looking. There will be times when it will seem like you have been denied by every employer in the world, but stick with it and do not quit because there is a job out there for you. Do not rule out the possibility of going into business for yourself. Let me re-phrase that. Do not rule out the possibility of creating your own "LEGITIMATE" business. Read books on starting and managing your own business. Research what resources are out there to help people start businesses. Then you may be in a position to give another person a break.

Do not Get Caught Up in the Hate

As far as they are concerned, there is no such thing as an "EX"-convict.

For whatever reason, there are people who have very bad opinions of people who have been convicted of a felony or been formerly incarcerated. They do not think a person in prison should ever get out of prison. Many times these people would hate you for one reason or another and some folks are just stupid like that. You may run into an employer who will give you a job, but want to pay you less than his other non ex-con workers. An employer may try to cheat you out of what you have legitimately earned by threatening to tell the PO things that could get you violated.

In general, there is considerable fear, prejudice, and suspicion of people with prison histories among the general members of society. In many cases, all people know about prison and the people in there is what they have seen on television and in the news. It is usually something negative. It is important to remember that many of the negative beliefs and perceptions that people have were earned legitimately by the past actions of some who have abused opportunities and perpetuated the myths. On the other hand there are many people who will want to help people with histories because maybe it gives them a good feeling to help a person who is down and out to get on his or her feet.

> Do your job and plan your next step out of a bad situation into a better situation.

You cannot control how and what other people think and you should not overly concern yourself with it. Do what you have to do to avoid trouble and do not get caught up in the drama. If you are on a job that is not working out for whatever reason, do not just quit the job before you have something else in place. Life in general is full of daily aggravations and petty people that you will have to deal with like everyone else. Do your job and plan your next step out of a bad situation into a better situation. Not everyone wants to see you do well. It is important to remember that "player-hating" does not always come from strangers. You will find that many people close to you, including family members, will do and say things meant to keep you from growing and moving beyond them.

Stay Within Your Circle of Possibilities

> For instance, do not waste your time filling out applications with the state police and avoid the banking field.

As a convicted felon with a prison history some career areas are not open to you. For instance, do not waste your time filling out applications with the state police, and avoid the banking field. In California, people with felony convictions are restricted from getting jobs as lawyers, doctors, nurses, or in real estate. Research the field of work you want to go into and make sure that the past will not disqualify you.

> Use the negative energy that people throw at you as fuel to ignite and reinforce your commitment and determination to keep going.

Halfway Houses

> The house rules and penalties of halfway houses and other community living type residence are usually of the strict, unforgiving, zero-tolerance type. Do not test the limits. Any inmate who gets the opportunity to go to a halfway house must set a good example! Do not do anything that would ruin the next man's chances of benefiting from the halfway-house experience.

Halfway houses are usually very good situations for a pre-parolee, if he can get it. Halfway Houses allow for a gradual transition from prison to parole. The traumas that come from being held years in prison isolation and then suddenly being thrown into society are not as severe on the parolee. There is time to adapt and adjust gradually. Halfway houses are also opportunities to save money, practice budgeting, establish banking accounts, and to prepare you for the day you are paroled.

PART TWO

How to Do Good After Prison

> Despite government support and resources, you can be successful after prison if willing to work hard for your life.

Doing time in prison does not require special skills or courage. Any common chump off the street can do time in jail. You do not have to be any kind of tough guy or thug. Anybody can do time in prison – one way or another.

On the other hand, it takes a special man or woman to make it – legitimately — on the outside after prison because there are so many things working against him, like few resources and little support for people after prisons. Despite government support and resources, you can be successful after prison if willing to work hard for your life. For those who have made the personal commitment to do the right things to stay out of prison, here are a few suggestions that can help make your transition smoother, with a better chance for success.

Relocate: Do not Go Back

> Sometimes it is difficult to stay focused when surrounded by familiarity. The distractions may come from old acquaintances in the street or from people and circumstances right there in your family home where you live.

Ultimately, every successful person – like every unsuccessful person - will not be so much a product of his environment, as much as he will be the product of the choices and decisions he makes within his environment. Their decision not to return to the old neighborhood – but instead to re-establish themselves in new surroundings – has played a major role in the personal success of many people who have failed again and again when they went back home after being in lookup.

Staying focused is important to any formerly incarcerated person trying to do the right things. Sometimes it is difficult to stay focused when surrounded by familiarity. The distractions may come from old acquaintances in the street or from people and circumstances right there in your family home where you live.

> As little as 25 to 35 miles between you and the old neighborhood can make a big difference in easing some of the pressures and temptations.

Whatever the distraction, sometimes it might be necessary to distance yourself from the situation so you can concentrate. For one reason or another, not everyone can just up and relocate to another city or state. As little as 25 to 35 miles between you and the old neighborhood can make a big difference in easing some of the pressures and temptations. Maintain communication and contact with your family, especially if you are fortunate enough to have supportive family ties that are strong and positive.

Some people go into prison homeless and alone and they leave prison homeless and alone. If that is your situation, than treat it as a positive because it may be easier for you to look for jobs and opportunities in places other than in your past community. Research and explore the possibilities. Family can also provide supportive environment for a person coming out to grow and find his way. Family may be the only acceptable situation that is available to provide a place for the parolee to live. In the end everyone has to do what he or she has to do. Just remember that when you find yourself in a bad situation you may have to suck it up and deal with it until you can do better. Lay out a plan and work toward it.

> Some men may feel that they do not need to relocate to be successful.

Once you leave from around the old way, stay away from around the old way. Start a new life in a new town with new people, with a new lease on life and a new attitude. Some men may feel that they do not need to relocate to be successful. Some men have been successful after prison living in their old neighborhood. For those who have tried everything else without success, relocating might make the difference.

> Remember to go through your parole officer before you start changing addresses or taking that trip to the Bahamas.

Cut all Negatives Ties

> It can be difficult to move away from the people you know and love, but you have to do what you have to do to be successful. Only then can you help anyone else.

It is very important to abandon all of the negative connections, associations, grudges, and vendettas from your past life. Just as you forgave yourself, you must forgive the errors in judgment and behavior of others. You will never go forward as long as you are holding on to the past. Just let it go! Rise above it and move beyond it.

Be very careful about whom you give your address or telephone number to. Tell your family not to give your telephone number or address to anyone. It can be difficult to move away from the people you know and love, but you have to do what you have to do to be successful. Only then can you help anyone else.

> You will never go forward as long as you are holding on to the past.

Meet People/Make Friends

> It may be wise to stay away from the wild clubbing party crowds.

Get out, mingle, do things. Night school, college classes, special interest courses, social groups and churches are ideal places to meet new people and to become involved in a variety of community activities.

It may be wise to stay away from the wild party crowds. Sometimes married men, living with their wife and kids, are a good choice of associates because they tend to be more stable and settled. Not always, however, because we all know that married men can be "out there" just like anyone else.

> If a person is formerly incarcerated, or so-called "ex-con", that is what he is and that is what he will be for the rest of his life – regardless of his latter success or the status he reaches in life.

Beware of people who appear to be drawn to you because you have a history. Unbelievably, there are many of those type people out there. Sometimes, people who admire you and want to be around you because your past life seems exciting and entertaining to them, may not want to see you stop doing those things. At the least, they will probably want to keep you talking about a life you have put behind you.

If a person is formerly incarcerated, or so-called "ex-con", that is what he is and that is what he will be for the rest of his life – regardless of his latter success or the status he reaches in life. A person should be proud of his past only in the sense that he was able to overcome it and begin the new life that he has. Once you have worked to create your new image it does not make sense to involve yourself with the wrong crowd and start the whole negative thing over again.

Listen to Your Gut

> Listen to that same gut feeling that used to warn you that someone was cop.

A friend and mentor who had a big influence on my life after prison would always tell me to use the same street knowledge and jail-wise savvy and instinct – that helped me survive in the bad worlds of the street and prison – to guide me in my straight life. Listen to your gut. It is the same gut feeling that used to warn you not to sell drugs to a stranger because he or she may be an undercover cop. That instinct will also let you know whether you are in a situation or environment or in the company of people who might threaten your future and freedom – if it is not already obvious to you. Listen to it. If it does not feel right, it probably is not right.

> If it does not feel right, it probably is not right.

Learn to Appreciate Home Life

> Spend time at home with her, cuddling or playing

> **games with the kids.**

Remember all the promises you made to the woman who has stuck by you through it all. Spend time at home with her, cuddling or playing games with the kids. Learn to appreciate the pleasure of being at home (when you are not working, etc.) with your woman and children, instead of in the streets with your boys. Share the joys and aggravations of raising the kids, and being married. If you have an argument with your woman, go to another room to cool off instead of storming out the door and leaving the house. There was nothing out in the streets worth jeopardizing your freedom and family over before you went to prison, and there is not anything good out there now. The difference is that the committed man realizes it now.

If you live alone, make your home comfortable and the place where you most want to be. Invite your woman to your place to watch a movie, or cook dinner for her. Get a cat to keep you company.

> **There was nothing out in the streets worth jeopardizing your freedom and family over before you went to prison and there is nothing good out there now. The difference is that the committed man realizes it.**

> *"Marriage is the roughest thing in the world. Nelson Mandela endured 27 years in a South African prison. But, when he got out it took only two years for his marriage to bust his ass."* – Comedian Chris Rock

Prepare for and Recognize Jail Lag

> He has not established a life on the street yet
> and he is having a few problems fitting into
> everyone else's.

The first few weeks or even months of freedom can be sweet for someone who has been locked up for a while. There is lots of love and attention and everyone is happy. The kids are glad that daddy is home because now he can take them places as he promised he would. The woman is happy because she can finally get her phone bill under control without all those damn collect calls from the prison. The formerly incarcerated person is just happy to be out of jail.

Then, somewhere around 60 to 120 days into post-incarceration the novelty wears thin and the real world kicks in. There haven't been any solid leads resulting from the job applications he put in around town and he spent the $200 gate money the prison gave him on the first weekend he was home taking the kids to Great Adventure. Everyone else has gone back to living his or her life as one did when he was away. Everyone except him, that is. His life, as he knows it, is back at the joint. He has not established a life on the street yet and he is having a few problems fitting into everyone else's.

> The stress of not being able to legitimately
> support oneself, let alone contribute meaningful
> financial assistance to the household budget,
> begins to wear on a persons pride and ego.

Then there's the inevitable arguments where his woman reminded him that she – and the kids – had a life while he was away that didn't stop just because he got out of prison. The kids are disrespecting him because the only place he has taken them since he has been home is Six Flags Great Adventure Theme Park, and that was months ago. Suddenly, he does not have the social status or control as he had inside.

The stress of not being able to legitimately support oneself, let alone contribute meaningful financial assistance to the household budget, begins to wear on a persons pride and ego.

A newly released person in that situation will feel depressed, bored, lonely, scared, disillusioned, embarrassed, broke, and sorry for oneself.

Next, anxiety and panic begin to set in and one may begin to question whether it is meant for them to be successful or whether prison is the ultimate fate regardless of how hard one tries. That is Jail Lag.

> **Jail Lag** is a term I made up. I borrowed the concept from the term Jet Lag. My definition of Jail Lag is: "The psychological and physiological disruption of a formerly incarcerated person's world caused by sudden travel from one extreme reality into another." Specifically, when going from years in prison to the streets, literally overnight. Kind of like jet lag with life threatening repercussions.

Jail Lag will actually make a man yearn for the security and leisure of prison life. He will miss the camaraderie he had with the other inmates in the prison. The structured time management, the constant choice of planned activities, the regular meals, the hot showers and the clean bed sheets twice a week. Most of all, a call you can go to for peace and solitude.

When a parolee begins to feel the presence of Jail Lag he should recognize that it is a dangerous and pivotal period in his life. Historically, people leaving prison have not handled the type of pressure and adversity that the real world dishes out very well. It is within this period of Jail Lag when a man is most vulnerable to making bad decisions – such as getting high or some other act of self-destructive surrender.

> Jail Lag will actually make a man yearn for the security and carefree of prison life. The card game camaraderie with the other inmates. The structured time management, constant choice of planned activities, regular meals, hot showers and clean bed sheets twice a week. Most of all, a call you can go to for peace and solitude.

Many formerly institutionalized people will experience some form of Jail Lag following their release into the real world. Being unemployed and without other positive outlets and interests can magnify the effects of Jail Lag, however, those with jobs will also probably hit a low point sometime after release from prison. That is why it is very important to stay active with positive activities, hobbies and interests. Try things you have never thought about doing before, like going to the museum or writing that novel.

> Bad times will come and go, so just hang in there. It will get better if you keep doing the right things and do not give up.

Professional Assistance and Counseling

> Do not wait until you are in trouble, because by then it may be too late. You have to seek and ask for help when you first begin to feel negative pressures and thoughts overwhelming you.

The majority of the technical violations that send parolees back to prison are drug related, such as failing a drug test. Drug counseling or personal counseling is something every parolee should consider even if not ordered as part of the parole conditions. Read the newspapers to find out what is going on in the community. Attend AA (Alcoholics Anonymous) or NA (Narcotics Anonymous) meetings where you can find support from others with whom you can talk. Get involved in community activities, sports teams, the church or other religious groups.

If you are not working yet go to a homeless shelter or a soup kitchen and put in a few volunteer hours each week. There is no greater medicine to cure the "Poor little ex-con trying to do the right things but who just cannot seem to get a break" blues, than to see others who are worse off than you are. Do things with your family and on your own.

> Many incarcerated people and, therefore, many formerly incarcerated people, suffer with mental health issues. Most times those issues are not addressed while the person is in prison.

Many incarcerated people and, therefore, many formerly incarcerated people, suffer with mental health issues. Most times those issues are not addressed in the prison. Search for resources and services in your home area where you may be able to get support. Begin to set up your support systems early.

Do not wait until you are in trouble, because by then it may be too late. You have to seek and ask for help when you first begin to feel negative pressures and thoughts overwhelming you.

> Go to a homeless shelter or a soup kitchen or senior center and put in a few volunteer hours.

Make Good Decisions

In my work over the years and, of course having been a former frequent parole violator myself, I have found that in many instances, a parole violator had the power and opportunity to make the right decision and did not.

Unlike in prison, there are going to be a number of serious decisions that a parolee has to make on a daily basis. Many of these decisions will affect directly whether the parolee continues his life of freedom or whether he goes back to prison.

In my work over the years and, of course having been a former frequent parole violator myself, I have found that in many instances, a parole violator had the power and opportunity to make the right decision and did not.

One bad decision, as I mentioned earlier, is doing drugs before a drug test. Maybe one night he decides that he is having too much fun at the club and stays out past his curfew. Maybe it is just failing to report to the PO when required to do so, because he did not feel like it. In essence, that parolee has made a formal request to be sent back to prison for a violation of parole or conditional release agreement. It is that simple.

Respect Women & Children

Any man who considers himself a man would be more sensitive to the abuse and humiliation that he puts his mother, and his woman, and his kids through every time they have to submit to the prison's visitor process just to see him.

Take time to consider the negative impact your presence in the prison has had on your family and loved ones. In many cases, the women and children of inmates suffer worse than does the man in jail.

Any man who considers himself a man would be more sensitive to the abuse and humiliation that he puts his mother, and his woman, and his kids through every time they have to submit to the prison's visitor process just to see him. Some correction officers tend to treat the family members of prisoners with the same disrespect and arrogance that they do toward inmates. It is ironic that many times the man in prison eats better, sleeps better, and has a much more fulfilling social life in prison than his woman and kids have on the street. Especially if the woman is trying to finance his comforts of incarceration by sending money and buying different items and food to send him while he is in prison. Think about the other people that you hurt when you go to jail. Respect and appreciate your family.

Think Long Term

> Live your life as though you expect to be out there forever.

Do not be afraid. Live your life as though you expect to be out there forever. Take out a loan, establish credit, start a business, get custody of your children, sign long term leases, join community groups and 401k plans. Your first loan does not have to be for a large amount. The important thing is that you can use it as a reference for future loans and credit. Department store credit cards are sometimes easier to obtain than major credit cards such as Visa or MasterCard, and they are good cards to begin a credit history. Just remember that you have to pay your bills on time or the whole point is moot.

Accumulate Stuff

> Remember, the stuff you accumulate should be
> stuff that you worked and paid for.

When you get your first paycheck, buy yourself
something. You will have bills to pay and you will pay
them. However, there is nothing more disillusioning
than working every day just to pay bills. Also, once you
have your favorite recliner and your big screen television
and your computer, it tends to be an incentive for you to
stay out there and do the right thing. It is harder to
jeopardize going back to the prison and losing the stuff
you have worked hard to gain. Remember, the stuff you
accumulate should be stuff that you worked and paid
for.

Raise Your Kids: Make Them Your Cause

> Do you know where your children are right now,
> this moment as you read this book?

Do you know that according to the U.S. Bureau of
Justice more than half of all the State and Federal
prisoners have children under 18 years old? The Bureau
reports that's about 800,000 parents locked down away
from their children.

Do you know that the Bureau statistics show that
more than 90% of the parents in prison are fathers?
(U.S. Bureau of Justice) Do you know where your
children are right now, this moment as you read this
book? Do you know where they are and what they are
doing at any time, around the clock, all week long?

No, you do not know. How could you? You are in the
joint and your kids are dying in the streets. Your son
could be the 12-year-old kid they busted with a loaded

gun in his pocket. Your kid might be the 14-year-old little girl shot in the head over a boy.

It is hard to imagine that there could be a person in prison who wants their sons and daughters to follow his/her footsteps, but that is exactly what is happening. It is not uncommon to have three generations– granddad, dad, and son – doing time in the same joint. Unless more men are there to guide and help raise their kids, the inner city and poor neighborhoods will continue to be the primary feeder source for the prison industry. Direct those much talked-about negative, pent-up feelings of hate for the prison system into an effort to denying it from consuming your children as it consumed you. Fatherhood is a great thing with many rewards. More daddies should try it. Only daddy can save their kids.

> It is hard to imagine that there could be a person in prison who wants their sons and daughters to follow his/her footsteps, but that is exactly what is happening.

Get involved in the schools, check homework, join the PTA and meet your children's teachers. Stay up on what your kids are into in school and in the neighborhood, and in the home. Encourage and challenge your children to read and exercise their minds. Make your children understand that education is important. Make them understand that getting their education is "non-negotiable" and that for them to complete school is fully expected.

Regulate how much television they watch. Buy your kids more books and learning toys. Set aside a time each day to turn off the television and read. Read with your kids and read to your kids. Every successful person needs a Cause to rally behind. If every man in prison came out and took a positive and active role in his kid's lives, he would benefit greatly. Barking threats at your kids over the telephone or in the visiting hall while you're sitting up in there wearing that bright orange jumpsuit is not going to do it. Before a man can talk the daddy talk he has to out walk the daddy walk.

> Daddy must save his kids!

Wrap It Up

> Kids can bring you much joy when you do it right. They can also bring you a slow painful death – in the form of child support payments.

Speaking of kids, you should wear a condom when having sex. This is not about catching a disease; it is about not catching any babies you are not willing and able to support. Making babies all around town is not manly. It is irresponsible and ignorant. A man having sex with a woman other than his wife should wear a condom to protect him and the woman he is with.

If you are a guy who just cannot control his roll, a vasectomy is an option. Do not make babies that you do not want. Make enough babies that you cannot afford and you may wish you had an STD instead. At least the disease will kill you in a few years and it will be all over. Kids can bring you much joy when you do it right. They can also bring you a slow painful death – in the form of child support payments.

Never Forget

> Be careful not to forget how it was in prison and how much you never, ever, want to go back.

The average man in prison has whined and complained to everyone who will listen about how finished he is with prison and the life of crime. It is the same song that he sang the last five times he was locked up. People are tired of hearing it. Be careful not to forget how it was in prison and how much you never, ever, want to go back.

Take Your Time

> There are always going to be things to work out and overcome.

Do not try to make up for lost years. Whatever time you spent in the joint is gone. Learn to appreciate living in the "now," while planning for your future. There are always going to be things to work out and overcome. Sometimes you have to commit to do something, and you will figure out the details later.

Vote and Get Politically Aware

> The laws on convicted felons voting rights vary from state to state.

Since you are going to be paying taxes and living the consequences of the people in public office – whether you believe in the system or not – you may as well vote. Do not be discouraged because the Republicans stole the 2000 presidential election by throwing away black folks votes in Florida. Turning out to vote even stronger next time is the best revenge. Vote with vengeance!

The laws on convicted felons voting rights vary from state to state. In some states, a formerly incarcerated person can vote once he completes parole and in other states, convicted felons lose their right to vote forever. Check the laws in your state. (See jointfx.com for specific voting and other state/federal disabilities of ex-felons.

Do not Play with the Authorities

> Some law enforcement officers take on a new
> personality when they find out that you are a
> convicted felon.

I bring this up because there are actualized and potential consequences of being a convict for the rest of his life that a man should expect and prepare for. For instance, I am always conscious of the fact that twenty years after leaving the joint and being a positive citizen I am still only a traffic stop away from misery. If I, or any other formerly incarcerated person, were pulled over by the wrong cop on a bad day and he/she runs my license through the computer, and my past history shows up, it could be ugly if the officer is in a bust-somebody's-ass mood.

Some law enforcement officers take on a new personality when they find out that you are a convicted felon. That is why it is important to avoid any kind of run-in with the police as much as possible. You may be stopped for an expired inspection sticker, but once your jacket is revealed you may wind up taking the rap for a burglary that went down in that neighborhood six months back. What I am saying is, do not play with the police.

Dress to Impress

> You do not need a suit all the time, if you are
> neat, and clean.

Always dress appropriately when you go to job interviews. Always wear a shirt and tie. A white shirt is most desirable but if you do not have a white shirt, any button up shirt with a collar will do. You do not need a suit all the time, if you are neat, and clean. Shine your shoes, wear a belt and put your hat on straight. On second thought, leave the hat at home with the head rag and bandana.

Tattoo Taboo

> If you have not started with extreme tattoos and body piercing on parts of your anatomy that are visible to the public, do not start

For best impression, avoid flashy jewelry, outlandish haircuts, or outrageous body piercing.

If you have not started with extreme tattoos and body piercing on parts of your anatomy that are visible to the public, do not start. If you have already done the tattoo thing, stop now. Look like a thug and you will probably be received as a thug.

Thrifty Shopping

> They are a perfect place to get started with a respectable business wardrobe and home furnishing.

Thrift stores and secondhand type stores, such as Goodwill and Salvation have good quality stuff like dress shirts, shoes, ties, jackets, and household item, at affordable prices. There is no shame in shopping at thrift and discount stores. They are a perfect place to get started with a respectable business wardrobe and home furnishing. Unless you tell him or her, nobody is going to know where you buy your stuff.

Fighting for Your Rights: A Person Victory

In 1995 I was employed with a State Division of Juvenile Services as the Superintendent of a 45-bed juvenile residential facility located in a South Jersey. One day a memo came out that said all Department supervisory personnel would need a Commercial Class Drivers License (CDL), to retain their titles. As a Superintendent, I was required to take the test so I took the test, passed the test, and got my CDL license.

A few months go by and I receive a letter from the NJ Motor Vehicles Services telling me that my CDL license had been suspended due to my past felony convictions. The notice said I had 21 days to submit a written appeal directly to the MVS Director, explaining why I felt my CDL should be restored.

Feeling confident that my past 16-plus years as an upstanding, positive, tax-paying member of society would speak for itself, in terms of my worthiness to possess a CDL, I sent in my appeal.

After another two weeks go by and I get a letter back from the MVS that basically said, it is nice that I was doing well and all, but the rules say that a convicted felon is prohibited from having a CDL license. The next level of appeal was to the NJ Office of Administrative Law, where I could go in front of a judge and state my case face-to-face. The MVS came into the court and dragged my name through the mud bringing up the past, but I won. The following is a brief review of the judge's decision in that case. (A full version of this decision is at www.jointfx.com)

"The Department of Corrections employed respondent (Mr. Jackson), in 1986, so apparently it made the determination that respondent was rehabilitated even then. It has been 19 years since respondent was involved in any criminal activity, and now at a mature age he has a position of responsibility and trust. He is charged with the supervision of 45 juvenile delinquents and the 24 staff members who manage the correctional facility. Surely, if he is responsible for every aspect of the daily care of these young people whom the courts have entrusted to him, he is responsible enough to transport them around the facility, to court appointments, etc. I CONCLUDE that the respondent has established himself as a responsible, productive citizen, totally rehabilitated and free from any adverse effects of the criminal activities in which he was involved 19 years ago. It is therefore ORDERED that that the notice of schedule suspension of bus/CDL privileges issued to respondent on September 22, 1993 is hereby RESCINDED and the within matter is DISMISSED WITH PREJUDICE.

A convicted-felon's past can, and will, come up in the most unsuspecting and embarrassing situations for you, and for your loved-ones, no matter how long you have been out doing good. There is no worse feeling then applying for insurance or a mortgage and The Big Question pops up on the application or in the interview, "Have you ever been arrested or convicted of a crime?" This is usually followed by, "If yes, please explain in detail. (Use extra paper if necessary.)" A convicted-felon can get a passport, but some countries will not let you in if they know you have a jacket. I know a few people who didn't find that out until they got to the customs in that country and answered "yes" to The Big Question on the form they give the in-coming tourists to fill out. Not every country asks, but it is good to find out before you get there. Do not let it get you down, just handle it and address it. I addressed it and won. I didn't address it by punching the DMV guy in the face, or threatening to kick his ass. I went through the proper channels, did my research, learned what I needed to do and I did it, and did it successfully.

> Always fight for your rights. Learn the system and use it to your advantage, the right way.

> *"A man can get used to anything and I had grown used to Robben Island (Prison in South Africa). I had lived there for almost two decades and while it was never a home... it had become a place where I felt comfortable. I always found change difficult, and leaving Robben Island, however grim it had been at times, was no exception. I had no idea what to look forward to."*
> Nelson Rolihlahla Mandela

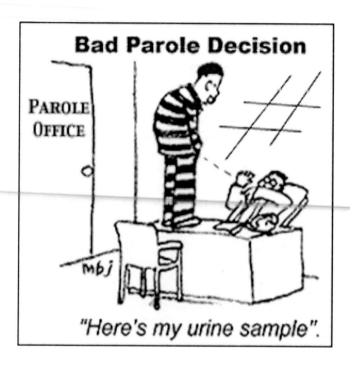

How to Do Parole

According to the U.S. Parole Commission, when someone is paroled, they serve part of their sentence under the supervision of their community. The law says that the U.S. Parole Commission may grant parole if (a) the inmate has substantially observed the rules of the institution; (b) release would not depreciate the seriousness of the offense or promote disrespect for the law; and (c) release would not jeopardize the public welfare.

To a parolee, and all those around him, life on parole can be inconvenient, restrictive, annoying, invasive, debilitating, undignified, and highly unforgiving. On the other hand, so is life in prison. Parole can be a better alternative to prison for those who do it right.

In reality, parole – like prison – is supposed to be a pain in your butt, a deterrent, and punishment. The successful person refuses to be thrown off his course or defeated by parole. The successful parolee turns the hassles of parole into a positive source of motivation and inspiration for himself.

It is extremely important for a parolee to understand, and never forget, that parole is a "conditional" liberty, with many conditions. Parole is an extension of incarceration. Parole does not mean freedom. Technically a parolee is still doing time – only on the outside. As a parolee you have no more "rights" than if you were still inside the prison.

Parole is also an opportunity not to be in prison. An opportunity and another chance to be with your family and an opportunity to have more freedom than if you were in the prison. Parole is also an opportunity and another chance for a man to do something worthwhile with his life. Many present and former parolees will agree that life on parole can be ten times tougher and more complicated than life in the joint. In many ways a parolee needs more intelligence, toughness and determination to be successful on parole than is needed to make it in the prison.

For example, parole officers have the authority to enter and search a parolee's home at any time, without a warrant, and confiscate anything he thinks is contraband. The police cannot even come into your house without a warrant. Well, the cops are not supposed to come into your house without a warrant.

It is one thing to have the prison guards trash your cell in a search for contraband. It is something altogether different to have a parole officer rummaging through your wife's underwear drawer during one of his unannounced searches. The transition from prison to the streets is something most men do not give the consideration that it warrants. There may also be limited prison sponsored resources that would help prepare a prisoner for a successful life on the street.

You have to be proactive and manage your own life. If you do not do it for yourself, it probably will not get done. It may sound like a small thing but the inability to manage time and habits has been the downfall of many capable, well-intentioned, and intelligent people. It takes willpower, determination, self-control, and responsibility to stay focused on the street because the distractions and temptations of daily life can swallow you up. A seemingly harmless moment of weakness can bring a parole violation and another all-inclusive iron vacation for you back at the joint.

Parole is unquestionably the biggest responsibility of a parolee. If you screw up on parole, nothing else really matters. Eventually the violations of parole that you commit will catch up with you and send you back to prison.

This book offers only a glimpse of the parole/conditional release programs out there. For more specific information about state or Federal parole/conditional release/probation, the parolee should contact the department in his or her area. Read the Parolee Handbook information, if your parole system has one, and memorize the COPs (conditions of parole) on your state's parole certificate. Not all states have a parole system, so obviously there will not be any "conditions of parole" in those states. In California there is no parole and prisoners usually serve their entire sentences in the joint. However, people released from prison in California are still subject to a "conditional release" period of post-incarceration supervision. In addition, the language and wording may vary from state to state; however, the principles are universal.

(See Appendix C for the parole authority specific to you.)

Do not Punch Him in the Face

Say you are a formerly incarcerated individual at your new job at the factory and one of your co-workers is this loudmouth, know-it-all type, who is always talking junk. One day this co-worker starts rattling off how all ex-cons are scum who should be shot and never let out of prison. "I can smell them a mile away," he boasts.

He is not talking about you, specifically. He does not even know that you were formerly incarcerated. It really does not matter who or what he is talking about to you, anyway. He could be talking about the space shuttle for all you care. You know he is a punk, you just do not like him and he is really getting on your nerves. What do you do?

1. Ask him to stop saying bad things about the guys in the joint?
2. Kick his ass? *(You know he cannot fight because he talks too much.)*
3. Tell the boss on him?
4. Sit back, take a deep breath, relax, close your eyes for a moment, and imagine him in the joint doing someone else's laundry?

The answer – *of course* - is "4".

Do not be kicking nobody's ass!
It is not worth the drama to react to all the ignorant people you are bound to run into every day. The important thing to remember is that no matter how well you are doing in the world there are going to be times when you are tempted to kick some ass.

The "Unannounced" Visit

It is 8 a.m. one Sunday morning and Joe X. Prison and his wife, Sherry, are in their apartment snuggled up in bed sleeping like two babies. The peace was abruptly interrupted by a hard knock at the door.

"BAM... BAM... BAM...!"
"JOE... JOE PRISON!"

Jolted out of his sleep by the loud noise and someone calling out his name, Joe sat straight up in the bed and immediately reached under his pillow for his shank. It has only been a couple of weeks since he got out and sometimes when he is startled out of his sleep it takes him a few moments to realize that he is not still in the joint sleeping with one eye open. After 7 years inside some habits were proving harder to break than others. Sleeping with his shank (a small screw driver) was one of them. Sitting there still half-asleep and confused, Joe's head begins to clear and get oriented. He looks over at his wife, who is still fast asleep.

"She would not have made it a week in the joint" he thinks to himself and smiles. *"She sleeps way too hard".*

"BAM... BAM... BAM...!"
"JOE... JOE PRISON!"

There it goes again. That one also woke Sherry, *"What was that Joe?"*

"The door baby" says Joe. *"Someone is at the door"*

"Well, who is it? Sherry asked, rubbing her eyes and rising up to rests on her elbows. *"I do not know anyone who would knock on people's doors like... wha... what in*

the world are you doing with that screwdriver in bed again? I thought I put that thing back in the toolbox where it belongs.

"*Yeah, whatever*" Joe mumbles under his breath, as he fumbles to quickly open his nightstand drawer and put the shank inside and then close the drawer again.

"*Huh?*" asked Sherry, cupping her ear and leaning over to hear better. "*What was that, Joseph?*"

"*You know I can't sleep without it under the pillow, baby*" Joe said as he throws back the covers and swings his legs over the side of the bed. "*If someone breaks in here while we're asleep you'll be glad I have that in here*"

"*That little screw driver against a gun?*" says Sherry as she lay back down and turns on her side and pulls the covers over her head. "*You crazy boy*"

"*Go back to sleep. I'll get the door*" Joe said.

Actually, he knew that she was right. His screwdriver may have been a prized shank inside, but it would be useless against anyone coming in with a gun. He just could not sleep without it under his pillow. He was working on it.

Joe slid into his slippers and stood up in the same motion. He grabs his robe and fumbles to put it on as walk out of the bedroom and down the hall to the door.

Joe had been doing the right things since getting out, but still his stomach muscles were tight and his mind was racing to remember anything he could have done to bring the police to his door that morning.

Things were going good, he thought. He had made his parole office visit last Tuesday and his next scheduled reporting day was not until the next Tuesday. It was every Tuesday. He was to start a new job in the morning. He had not gotten high, drank alcohol, committed any crimes since he had been home. He had done everything he was supposed to do.

"BAM... BAM... BAM...!"
"JOE... JOE PRISON!"

Joe cannot think of anything out of order, and frankly, now he has an attitude. If it was not the authorities than who the hell was knocking at his door and yelling like that?

Joe, slowed his pace briefly, as he considered about going back to get the shank. He decided against that.

"YEAH, WHO IS IT?" Joe's voice boomed at the door. He did not go right up to the door and stood to the side away from directly in front of the door - just in case. It was an old habit from the old days when people were likely to shoot through the door at him.

"OFFICER D. MANN, FROM STATE PAROLE, TO SEE JOE X. PRISON", came the voice from the other side of the door.

Joe recognized the voice now and rolled his eyes as he opened the door. There, sure enough, looking like a Marine on his way to war was his parole officer, BD Mann.

BD always dressed the same way. Green, or some times tan or gray army camouflage fatigues, always tightly pressed and creased. His pants tucked into spit shined, tightly laced and zippered Doc Martin boots. A black tee shirt (2 sizes too small to accent his biceps had "Parole" printed in bright orange fluorescent letters on the front and back. He wore multiple thick black leather belts and holsters crisscrossing his waist, shoulders, and chest, with guns, walkie-talkies, handcuffs, pepper spray, bullets, a flashlight, flares, and stuff that looked like hand grenades, water canteen, screw drivers, wrenches, hammers, and God knows what other stuff hanging from them. He topped it all off with a NY Yankee baseball cap turned backward.

"Mr. Prison, how you doing?" The parole officer brushes past Joe and enters the apartment before he was invited in. *"Did I wake you?"*

Joe stuck his head out the door to look into the hallway and see if any of his neighbors were looking. Then he closed the door, pausing a moment to close his eyes and takes a slow deep breath, *"Yeah, you woke me and probably the whole damn, neighborhood!"*

That is what Joe would like to have said. Instead he put up a polite smile and says, *"I wasn't expecting you today, BD. What brings you here this morning?"*

"Well, I was in the neighborhood and thought I'd stop up and see you. We'll count this as one of your random home checks," said *BD,* his eyes scanning the room wall to wall and floor to ceiling, like he was sizing up Joe's crib for a heist. *"You know we have to have at least one unannounced home visit every..."*

BD stopped in mid-sentence. He had stopped eyeing the room and was getting an eyeful of Sherry, who had gotten out of bed and was standing there in her robe and slippers, her arms folded tightly across her chest. Her eyes met Joe's and Ray Charles could see that she was mad. She had endured years of this in the prison visiting halls and she did not want it in her home.

BD was not a bad guy; in fact, Joe thought that he was a decent guy, as parole officers go. He was a pain-in-the-ass, but he was known to be fair. He would let a guy have a few small transgressions every now and then if you were trying. He also would not hesitate to lock your butt up, if you were caught wrong. BD had been in the Marines for many years, most recently as a reserve. He had just returned from a 7-month stint in Iraq that turned in to 12-moths 60-days before he was supposed to come home. The joke among his colleagues that he wore the same outfit to Iraq and was better equipped than the other soldiers in his unit.

BD knew everyone thought that he was eccentric, but he didn't care. He did everything by the book and could quote you the parole codes like saying his name. When BD started with the "routine" questions at Joe's weekly parole office visits they became anything but routine. BD left no stone unturned. He would sometimes want such intricate details of where Joe was and what exactly he was doing at a specific time that Joe began keeping a diary to record his daily activities and contacts with BD.

During on office visit Joe jokingly asked BD if he was secretly a former interrogator at Abu Ghraib Prison. BD took it as a compliment.

"Uhhhhh, this is my wife, Sherry. Honey, this is BD Mann, the parole officer" Joe says mostly to break the tension.

"Yeah, I met the lady when I came here to do your pre-parole investigation". BD began walking towards Joe's wife with his hand extended to shake her hand, *"How are you, Mrs. Prison...?"*

Sherry kept her armed folded tight and kept her death stare on Joe. He could tell that his wife was not happy with him about this loud, obnoxious man being there on account of him.

BD must have picked it up also because he quickly turned around and went right to his business with Joe.

"So Joe, how's it going? Any problems since I last saw you? Any contact with the police? Did you make that appointment for a drug evaluation? You ready to start your new job tomorrow? Someone told me that they saw you in the old neighborhood last week. I know your mother lives there but you need to try and stay away from that area."

"No, no problems. Yes, appointments are made. I start work tomorrow at 8 o'clock. I took my mom shopping last week, that's why I was there. Everything is good with me."

BD continued to check out the Living room and Joe found himself looking around nervously for anything out of order. BD walked over and picked up a half smoked cigar sitting in an ash tray on the coffee table, sniffs it a couple of times and puts it back into the ash tray. Then he picked up 4 empty soda cans sitting on the table, one at a time, and sniffs each one.

"Have a party last night, Joe?" BD asks sarcastically while flipping open the lid of an empty pizza box

"We had a couple of friends over for my birthday", Joe responds.

It was no big deal, but Joe's voice cracked and he stuttered as if he were lying.

"How about you...?" BD asked as he walks over and stands looking into the kitchen. *"Did you have anything else? You know you're restricted from drinking alcoholic beverages or using illegal drugs... you know... happy birthday, by the way"*

Joe looked over and his little son and daughter had come out of their bedrooms and were standing in their pajamas next to mommy rubbing their eyes as if they cannot believe that there is this strangely dressed man standing in their living room like he is taking over. All eyes were on Joe.

Joe felt frustrated, humiliated helpless, powerless, ashamed and mad as hell, all at the same time. It is one thing to deal with this scrutiny inside the prison, and completely another while standing in your own living room in front of your family. Joe understood the big picture and what was at stake so he remained polite.

"Yeah BD, I know.... I know all that" Joe said dryly through his intentionally fake looking smile. *"I don't drink or use drugs and you know that, Mann."*

Joe, 34 years old, did 7 years for heroin distribution and claims he never used a drug in his life. He would get a little touchy when people associated him with using drug, although he did used to smoke reefer. Joe didn't count reefer as a drug *("God made it")*.

"Who is that man, mommy?" Joe's son said 'mommy' but his eyes were looking at Joe for the answer.

"Just somebody to see Daddy. Come on, let's go back in the room while daddy takes care of his business", mommy says as she turns and begins to shoo the kids into her bedroom.

As the door closes behind them Joe hears his daughter say, *"Why does that man have all those bullets, mommy?"*
And his wife says, *"Ask your daddy when he comes in. Right now, go brush your teeth."*

"Listen, BD, do you think we could have done this at another time in the day. It's Sunday and my family and I were asleep", Joe says, not hiding his annoyance anymore.

"Well like I said Joe, I was in the area. We got to make four face to face home visits a month, so... oh, by the way..."

BD reaches into one of the oversized cargo pockets on the leg of his combat fatigues and pulls out a black plastic bag. He tears it open along the top and takes out a small clear plastic jar with a yellow screw on cap and hands it to Joe; *"While I'm here I might as well get a urine sample from you for your drug test."*

Joe looked down at the little plastic bottle and something snapped in his mind, *"Listen, you little weasel. First you bust up in my home like I'm hiding Osama bin Laden up in here, wake up my family and probably all the neighbors, you humiliate and disrespect me in front of my wife and kids, and then you think I'm going to piss in a bottle? Get... get the hell out of here before I.... your ass is lucky that my wife made me leave my shank in the bedroom"*

Fortunately, it was "inside" Joe's mind that snapped. In real life Joe politely took the little bottle and went into the bathroom and peed into it. Since he had not gone since waking up that morning, his specimen flowed with such force that it spilled over the rim of the jar. Joe rinsed off the jar and dried it with a paper towel. When he came out of the bathroom BD was standing there wearing latex gloves and a face mask covering his nose and mouth, his arms extended out in front of him, holding the plastic bag open with both hands for Joe to drop the sample into. Once safely sealed in the bag, BD pulled down the facemask, but he leaves on one glove on to handle the bag for transfer to his vehicle downstairs.

"Since your family is not dressed I won't ask to look in the bedroom, this time" he said turning towards the door. *"I'll see you in the office next Tuesday, right? You stay outta trouble."*

Joe was already standing there with the door open.

"Yeah, thanks, for the consideration" Joe replied trying not to sound too sarcastic. *"I'll be there Tuesday. Oh, by the way, BD. You have my number, right? Maybe you can call ahead next time and I'd be happy to open the door. We can do this without waking my family and neighbors"*

"Call ahead?" BD said, stopping to make one last glance of the living room for anything he may have missed. . *"Well, that would defeat the whole purpose of the 'unannounced' thing... but I'll see what I can do."*

Joe closed the door behind BD and he could hear the crackle of BD's walkie-talkie being turned on and echoes off the cinderblock walls in the hallway,

"Senior Parole Officer, BD Mann leaving parole subject's, Joe X. Prison's, residence at 1313 Mockingbird Lane, Apartment number 666, complete home check – Ten-Four. Will arrive at next subject's residence in approximately... "

As Joe walk towards the closed bedroom door where his family is waiting, he first feels weak and sad but immediately a wave of commitment and determination lifts his spirit and Joe promised himself to do whatever it takes to never again put himself or his family through the hell and humiliation of prison and parole ever again!" Now he has to convince his wife and reassure his children. But, first he went into the kitchen and made waffles for everyone. Waffles with the family on Sunday morning and life is good again.

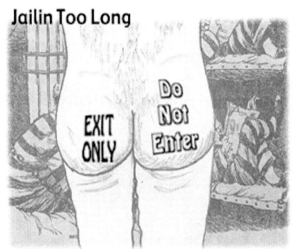

So far Lenny's tattoos were keeping the
wolves off his back.

Part 4

Good Parole Habits

Every parolee has to decide for himself whether the aggravations of parole are worth the pay-off of not being inside the prison serving his sentence. If you decide that the streets are for you, take a look at the following advice and information that can help you do well on parole.

Recognize the PO

The best way to introduce the topic of Parole to a parolee is to explain role and status of the Parole Officer, and/or the Probation Officer (PO). The PO may be the single most powerful and, influential, person in your life while on parole. The sooner you realize and accept that, the better off you will be.

The PO's primary job responsibility is to protect the public from you, the convicted felon. The way POs do that is by making sure that every parolee under his/her supervision is obeying the conditions and mandates of the parole agreement.

Some POs will give a parolee a little rope, and some will be in your stuff like bread in the prison meatloaf.

Just like parolees, POs come in all shapes, sizes, and mentalities. A parole officer is a law enforcement officer with all the powers to arrest and lock up a parolee thought to have violated conditions of parole. In most states, POs carry guns, handcuffs and mace and stuff and they have law enforcement powers.

When a parolee finds himself standing before a judge, or Parole Revocation Hearing Officer, the PO has a powerful voice in the decision whether a parolee goes back to prison or if he gets another chance at life on the outside. Develop a good relationship with your PO and there will be mutual benefits for everyone.

Think "Win-Win"

Do not approach your relationship and interaction with the P.O. as a competition that must produce a winner and a loser. Get over that mindset. You must approach parole and lives in general with a "win-win" attitude – not win-lose. You win and the parole officer wins. You win and your family wins. You win and your employer wins. If everyone wins, everyone is happy. Imagine how sweet your life would be if everyone in it was happy.

Look at it from the parole officer's point of view. POs carry extremely high caseloads. It is not uncommon for a single parole officer to have 50 or more parolees under his or her supervision at any given time. It is an awesome, if not impossible, task for one person to supervise and monitor that many people on a regular and thorough basis. If a parole officer gets a parolee that he or she does not have to be concerned about, they may relax and stay off your back – as long as you are showing that you are doing the right things.

The parole officer can adjust the level or intensity of your parole supervision according to how well – or not –he or she thinks you are doing. You can be required to report to the parole officer several times a week or you can be required to give a phone call every 30 days. How parole affects a parolee's life is determined by how the parolee handles the situation.

Know the Rules

You must read and understand exactly what your parole certificate states as to what you are expected to do and not do. Claiming ignorance of your parole conditions and responsibilities is not an acceptable defense against a violation of parole (VOP).

The PO may not tell you about your rights, or even respect them; however, parolees sometimes have certain rights and protections under the law. A parolee should also know what his rights are as a parolee. For instance, a person being accused of a violation of parole or conditional release has a right to a hearing and to be represented by an attorney at that hearing. Sometimes a state appointed attorney is assigned if the parolee is indigent, or broke.

Your experience with court appointed attorneys or public defenders as a defendant may be mixed. Sometimes it is not worth the delay in having a parole hearing to wait for an attorney to be assigned for the little effect and interest they tend to have on your case. It is much more effective for a parolee if he understands everything about his parole. This way, you can be effective if you have to defend yourself against violations.

Talk to Your Parole Officer

Find out exactly what the PO expects from you so that there are no surprises. If there is something you do not understand, or have any question about, talk to the PO about it until you do understand.

Show Due Respect to Authority

You must overcome any deep-rooted problems you may have "authority figures." That is probably much of the reason why you ended up in prison – no one could tell you what to do. Be it your parents, a teachers, a social worker, the police, the Judge, whomever. Your instinct is usually to battle and do it your way, with no consideration for compromise.

It is counter-productive for a parolee to get into playing head games with the PO. Leave the thug attitude back at the Prison. Rise above it, and move beyond it.

In reality, the PO is not much different from any of the other various "authority figures" of one type or another who will be lurking in the shadows of your life telling you what to do. Be it your PO, your employer, your wife, or whoever. If a parolee has difficulty dealing with a parole officer, he will probably continue to have difficulty in life.

In most cases, the PO is just doing his or her job, not deliberately trying to make your life miserable. Easy supervision for the PO means easy supervision for the parolee. Never forget that your goal is to successfully complete parole, at all costs.

Keep Your Reporting Dates

Be responsible! Keep your scheduled reporting appointments with the PO. Try not to miss reporting dates, but if for some reason you cannot avoid missing an appointment call the PO and let him know. Volunteer to come in the next day or at the next possible opportunity. Stop by or call the parole office between appointments, every now and then. Let the parole officer see that you are doing okay and that you have nothing to hide.

Keep Notes & Records

Whenever you go to the parole office or call the parole office and your PO is not there, leave your name and information with the person you speak to and ask them to tell the PO that you called. Also make sure you get the name of the person you spoke to and write it down. Parole officers keep detailed chronological records of all contacts, attempted contacts, and interactions with each parolee under their supervision. That is how POs prove what they say happened actually happened. It is a good idea for parolees to keep a small ledger to record all of your contacts and interactions with parole. It could come in handy one day.

Obey the COPs (Conditions of Parole)

Read, memorize, learn and understand the conditions of your parole. Then comply with them 100%. You may think that there are too many restrictions and demands on your time and energy. There will probably be "special conditions" ordering you to participate in drug counseling, mental health counseling, community service, curfews or something else that you may not feel that you need. Do not fight it. Just do it. Prove that you do not need it. Turn the experience into a positive one and make it work for you. It probably will not hurt you. You may even learn something useful.

Keep the PO Informed

Keep the PO informed of any changes in your status and of any problems that you are experiencing or that you anticipate. If you change addresses, get a speeding ticket or plan to leave the state you must inform your parole officer. If you do not, it is an automatic violation. Parole is extremely personal relationship between a parolee and the parole officer. You cannot get more personal than peeing in a cup (drug testing) while someone looks at you. However, do not become offended and take things personal. Communication solves and prevents many problems.

A Few Bad Parole Habits

Besides the obvious things like committing another crime, passing "hot urine" and not showing up at reporting time, here are a few things you might not want to do if you are on parole:

☹ DO NOT... Show up at the parole office wearing a head rag, stocking cap, or bandanna.

☹ DO NOT... Pull up to the parole office on reporting day two hours late in a brand new Honda Accord when the parole officer knows that you do not have a driver's license or a job.

☹ DO NOT... Show up at the parole office with 50 pounds of gold chains and rings adorning your body. Especially when the parole officer knows that you do not have a job.

☹ DO NOT... Show up at the parole office with five of your homeboys tagging along. Especially when the parole officer had three of them on parole last year.

Jailin Too Long

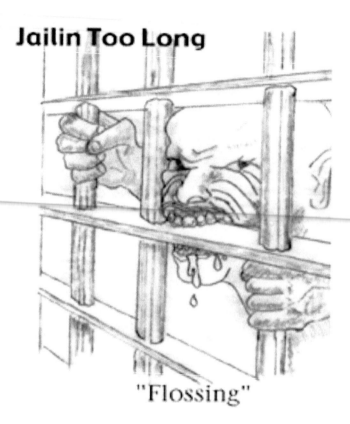

"Flossing"

PART 4

The "COPs" (Conditions of Parole)

The only person with more lame excuses than a man in prison is a parole violator on his way back to prison. As a parole violator myself back in the day, I probably tried them all in my attempt to avoid having parole violated. Today, as a parole violations hearing officer I hear them all from the parole violators who come before me.

Most parole violators can give you 1,001 reasons why it is not their fault that they violated their parole. Yet, in almost every case of the parole violators I talk to there was a conscious decision made by the parolee to behave in a manner that he knew would result in a violation of parole and his possible return to prison. A parolee knows that the parole officer takes a urine sample every week to test for drugs, but goes out and uses drugs or alcohol anyway or he stays out after curfew or does not go to reporting.

The United States Department of Justice says that 82% of parolees who are violated and returned to prison are returned for drug related technical violations. That is why I thought it was important to go over some of the rules and guidelines that a parolee or conditional releasee will be expected to live under.

Under state supervision, they are usually called Conditions of Parole ("COPs"), or Conditional Release Guidelines, or, in the case of the Federal government, the "Standard Conditions of Release".

I just refer to them as the "COPs" because these rules will police a parolee's every movement while he is under parole supervision. The COPs spell out exactly what the parolee is expected to do, when he is to do it, where it will be done, how it will be done, how long it will be done, and with whom it will be done while on parole.

There are generally two basic types of COPs

1. **General/Standard COPs** are the rules that appear on every virtually every State and Federal parole/release certificate for every parolee.

2. **Special" COPs** are conditions that may be added in addition to the standard general conditions to address the specific needs and concerns of each individual parolee. For example, a person who commits a sex offence may have a special condition stating that he must stay away from places where there are children or women.

There could also be special conditions ordering a parolee to attend mental health counseling, or drug counseling. Some "special" conditions of parole are also standard on all parole certificates. A stipulation that a parolee "must seek and maintain employment" is an example of a special COP that may be standard on all parole certificates.

A parole officer can also add special conditions at any time while a parolee is under parole supervision. Special conditions are where the PO gets specific in detailing what, when, where, how, and with whom – that is your life while on parole.

3. **Probable Cause and Revocation Process**; A parolee may be entitled to a probable cause or pre-disposition type hearing with a representative of the parole governing board that would determine whether parole will actually be revoked or not. In many instances, parolees are found not to be in violation of the conditions of parole as the parole officer has

charged. Sometimes a Parole Revocation Hearing Officer determines that the parolee has violated one or more conditions of parole but not seriously or persistently enough to send the parolee back to prison. In many of those cases the parolee is released from custody to continue on parole. When a parolee gets reinstated on parole by the parole board it may appear to be a victory for the parolee. In reality, a parolee could spend weeks, even months, in jail waiting for the process to take its course. That is why every parolee should try to avoid complications and misunderstandings that may cause him to become caught up in the red tape of the criminal justice system.

Frequent Violator Quote: *"Most of these violations happened months ago and the PO knew about them. Why didn't she violate me then?"*

The PO does not have to violate a parolee the first, second, or even the third time an act is committed that constitutes a violation. For example, you may not get violated and sent back to the joint the first time you break curfew, or the second time you miss a reporting appointment. Be certain, however, that when the PO does move to violate you, all of the past parole indiscretions that you thought you got away with will be listed in your violation. If the PO allows you to make a few mistakes without violating you, consider it a favor.

On the other hand, violating just one COP, just one time, can be grounds for the parole officer to issue a parole arrest warrant - the first step in having a parole revoked and the parolee sent back to prison.

The following are examples of General Conditions of Parole that may be found on a certificate of parole or conditional release agreement. For this book I have used examples from the New Jersey Parole Board certificate, which, for all intent and purposes, are the same as other State and Federal rules.

A Parolee must obey all laws.

It is appropriate that this COP be placed up front and number one, because it all begins and ends here. Obeying the law is the most important key to not only successfully completing parole but also for staying out of prison in the future. If a parolee is still dabbling in illegal activity while he is on parole – or not on parole – nothing else he does will matter. It will just be a matter of time before he is busted and headed back to prison with new charges, parole violations, or both.

Sometimes a parolee can only be found in violation if he is actually convicted of a new crime while on parole. An arrest or even an indictment for criminal activity is not always enough for a PO to arrest a parolee for violation of this COP. To be found in violation of this COP, the parolee must be convicted in a court of law or plead guilty to criminal charges in a court of law.

Unless given other instructions, a Parolee must report to Parole immediately after being released from the prison.

When released on parole, the first responsibility of a parolee is to contact the parole officer. Nothing, but nothing, is more important than getting with the PO when the PO is expecting you. An unbelievable number of parolees are violated and returned to jail within days of being paroled because they went to get high with their friends, or get laid, instead of checking in with the PO when they first got released. If you are not expected to get home until late in the day, you may be required to contact the PO the next day, or on Monday, in cases where you are paroled on a Friday. If something legitimate prevents you from getting to the parole, make sure to call and let the PO know what is up. It is unwise to screw up the very first visit.

Make the right decisions and take care of your responsibilities from the door.

A Parolee must notify his Parole Officer immediately after any arrest or contact with Law Enforcement.

Plainly and simply put, if you come into contact with the police, the courts, or any other legal or law enforcement situation, in any way, at any time while you are on parole, you must tell your parole officer about it immediately. An arrest may not be enough to put you in violation of your parole, however, not telling your PO about it is quite sufficient to send you back to prison. Avoid the drama that will surely play out if the PO finds out about what you have been up to from other sources in the street or on the police wire.

In real life there are many situations and circumstance that would prevent a parolee from getting in touch with the PO from lockup, especially if you only get one phone call. Still you should make the effort. If arrested and locked up in the municipal or county jail let them know that you are on parole and that you need to contact your PO.

Of course, this is all assuming that the parolee is using his or her real name and not using an alias. If a parolee is not using his real name, he most likely will not be calling the PO to say that he is busted.

Frequent Violator Quote: *"I couldn't call the PO from the jail to let him know that I was there because the jail only allows collect phone calls and the PO does not accept collect calls."*

Many, if not most, parole offices accept collect telephone calls from parolees. Make sure your parole office does not accept collect calls before you try to use this one. If the PO is not in when you call, leave your name with the person who answers the phone. Get that person's name before you hang up, in case you have to prove that you made the call. Write your information down on paper and put it in a safe place.

Frequent Violator Quote: *"I wasn't guilty of the charges so I didn't feel that I had to tell the PO that I was arrested or locked up."*

It does not matter whether you are guilty of the charges or not. As a parolee, you must tell the PO that you were arrested or if you get a traffic ticket or a jaywalking summons, or whatever, while still under parole supervision.

Frequent Violator Quote: *"I didn't tell the PO about the arrest because it was an old warrant for unpaid traffic ticket that I got before I was on parole."*

Remember, a parolee must tell the PO everything!

A Parolee must immediately notify the PO upon issuance of an order against him/her, or an order establishing bail in a criminal matter or offense arising out of a domestic violence situation.

In the event that someone, such as your wife, ex-wife, girlfriend, boyfriend or the young woman down at the 7-11, who has told you several times that you do not have a shot, has a restraining order lodged against you let the Parole Officer know immediately.

Frequent Violator Quote: *"I know that the restraining order said that I was not suppose to go within 500 feet of her, but we made up and she invited me over to her place."*

A Parolee must comply with any condition established within the respective order until the appropriate court dissolves the order or until a condition is modified or discharged by the appropriate court.

A restraining order usually comes in the form of a judge's order whereby a party (in this instance, the parolee), is required to do, or to refrain from doing, certain acts. Coming within a certain distance of another person or contacting that person in any way, (say your wife, your girlfriend, or a past victim) is an example. The party that fails to adhere to the injunction faces civil or criminal penalties and may have to pay damages or accept sanctions for failing to follow the court's order. In some cases, breaches of injunctions are considered serious criminal offences that merit arrest and possible prison sentences and violation of parole.

Frequent Violator Quote: *"Yeah, I knew she had filed a restraining order, but she invited me over."*

No one, except a judge, can modify or remove a restraining order once it has been issued. Not even the person who filed the complaint. All parties involved must obey the restraining order until a judge discharges it. Violation of this order is the cause of many parole violations resulting in parole being revoked

A Parolee must obtain approval of the parole officer for any change in residence.

A standard prerequisite to an inmate being released on parole is having an "approved residence." This is the place where the parolee will live when paroled. The residence is usually visited by the PO for inspection and evaluation as an appropriate place for the parolee to live. Once an address has been approved, the parolee cannot move or change his address without the pre-approval of the PO.

Frequent Violator Quote: "I didn't move out of my approved address. I was just sleeping at my girlfriend's house every night."

If you are not sleeping at your approved address – and doing so without the knowledge and approval of the PO – you are in violation of your parole. Even if you go home to change clothes every morning. Unless the PO gives permission to stay elsewhere, a parolee must sleep at the approved home.

A Parolee must obtain approval of the parole officer for any change in employment location.

Every able adult parolee must get a job as soon as possible after he or she is paroled. It is usually added as a 'special' COP on the parole certificate. Occasionally the Parole Board requires that an inmate obtain the promise of a job on the outside before they will grant him parole. Once you get that job, you have to obtain permission before you leave that job for any reason.

Frequent Violator Quote: *"I didn't quit the job. I got fired from my job. I was looking for another job and I planned to tell the PO after I found one".*

If you are fired or leave to start another job you must tell the PO, right away.

A Parolee must first obtain approval of the parole officer before leaving the state of his approved parole residence.

You must not for any reason leave the state in which they were paroled for any reason or period of time without the explicit permission of the PO. Not to go shopping, visit gamily or friends, or to take your kids to an amusement park. You must get permission from the Parole Officer. Get it in writing for your own protection.

A Parolee cannot own or possess any firearm or weapon for any purpose.

Is there anyone who does not understand NO GUNS? Many different things can qualify as a "weapon". Obviously, guns, knives, and the like are considered weapons. However, it would not be likely that a parolee would be violated for a steak knife he has in his kitchen or for the baseball bat in his bedroom closet. However, if caught with those same items in his pocket, or on his person, outside the home, then they are far more likely to be considered weapons.

The important thing to remember here is that unlike general COP #1, for the violation of illegal weapons possession to be applied it is not necessary for a parolee to be convicted, or arrested by the police or even formally charged in a court of law.

Frequent Violator Quote: *"It wasn't mine."*

A Parolee cannot not use, possess, or distribute a controlled dangerous substance, or CDS

That includes things like marijuana, heroin, crack, or, in some cases, alcohol, and of course all the other goodies that show up in the urine of many parole violators sent back to prison.

> Drug testing is to parole what dirty urine is to a parole violation. They are absolutes. They go together. Do drugs, do time!

Failed drug tests and drug related issues accounted for eighty-two percent of the technical violations that sent people back to prison. (U.S. Bureau of Parole)

If you are taking prescribed medication keep the bottle, and let the PO know what you are taking before giving the urine sample. It is better to avoid any potential problems.

Frequent Violator Quote: *"I didn't use any drugs. The cocaine must have gotten into my system through my skin while I was bagging it up to sell."*

Frequent Violator Quote: *"I was in my friend's car and they were smoking reefer. I must have breathed in some of the smoke."*

Frequent Violator Quote: *"I had a toothache and my girlfriend gave me one of her prescription painkiller pills that must have had something in it."*

Frequent Violator Quote: *"I was stressed out because me and my girl had an argument. I smoked some crack to feel better."*

Sometimes it is better to exercise your right to remain silent and just shut up!

A parolee cannot associate with anyone who has a criminal record unless given permission by the PO.

If you must associate, does it with positive minded people, whether they are formerly incarcerated or not.

A parolee cannot enter into any agreement to act as an "informer" or special agent for any law-enforcement agency.

That's right, no snitching activity, without the permission of your PO.

A parolee must pay any fines, restitution and penalties and Lab
Fees imposed by the sentencing court and/or State Parole Board.

A parolee's discharge or release from parole supervision at the end of his sentence can be held up if there are outstanding fines, fees, etc., owed by the parolee. This usually pertains specifically to fines, fees, lab fees, etc. that were imposed by the court in relation to the original conviction and sentence. This does not include any fines, from traffic tickets, or that the parolee may have accumulated from unrelated sources before or during his parole supervision – unless, if possibly for some reason, those unrelated fines were written in a 'special' COP. Just pay your bills. It is always possible to set up a reasonable payment plan with the PO.

Frequent Violator Quote: *"The parole officer never said anything about the fines, so I thought I didn't have to pay."*

Know and understand all of the responsibilities of your parole, including fines, fees, etc. It is up to you to see that they are taken care of. Just because the PO does not hassle you about every small detail of your parole responsibilities does not mean these responsibilities will go away.

Any Parolee convicted of a "sex crime" must register with the appropriate law enforcement agency.

Someone who has committed a sex offense must register with the police department in the community where he is going to live. Fail to register and you will go back to the Joint.

Someone who has committed a sex offense must also walk a tight line on parole. They tend not to get the breaks that a non-sex-offender might get. When they are being considered for parole, sex offenders are more closely scrutinized than most other offenders. Someone who has committed a sex offense is also more closely monitored and scrutinized by parole officers.

A parolee must permit confiscation by Parole Officer of any materials which your Probation Officer believes may constitute contraband in your possession and which your Probation Officer observes in plain view in your residence, place of business or occupation, vehicle(s) or on your person.

The PO can enter and search a parolee's home, workplace, car, pockets, and whatever else he wants to search at any time. The PO also can confiscate anything he feels is inappropriate.

A Parolee must waive extradition to the state of his or her parole from any other jurisdiction in which he or she is arrested and detained for violation of parole status.

A Parolee is expected not to contest any effort by any jurisdiction to return the parolee to the state of his parole. This means that in the event you are arrested in a different state than that in which you have been paroled, and if there is a parole violation warrant waiting for you in your home state, the authorities would appreciate it if you would return voluntarily and face your parole violations like a man. If you try to fight extradition, another violation can be tacked onto the others.

JAILIN TOO LONG

"Tyrone, do you have to yell out, 'this is for my dogs back on D-block', everytime we make love?"

APPENDIX A

Employment Information Handbook

Additional information about the Bureau of Prisons offender transition program, including the dates of future job fairs and a copy of the Mock Job Fair Handbook can be obtained from Federal Bureau of Prisons, Inmate Transition Branch, Washington, DC 20534   202-305-3860, 8128, 3553.

The following is the Table of Content of the full version of the Employment Information Handbook.

1. Purpose
2. What Should I Do to Prepare for Release?
3. What about Federal Programs to Help Ex-offenders?
4. What about State and Federal Jobs for Ex-offenders?
5. State Jobs
6. Federal Jobs
7. What about Loans and Grants?
8. What Programs are Sponsored by the U.S. Department of Labor?
9. One-Stop Employment and Training Services
10. Job Search
11. Physical and Mental Disability Employment and Training Services
12. National Internet Resource Link
13. Suicide Hot Lines
14. Adult Training Program
15. Native American Employment and Training Program
16. Senior Workers Employment Program
17. Senior Workers Employment Program
18. Employer Tax Credit Programs

Preparing for Release

You should start preparing for release as early in your sentence as possible. This should include an assessment of your career objectives, completion of all education and vocational training programs offered by the prison, resolution of any substance abuse issues that you may have, and development of a realistic post release plan.

Parents should participate in parenting programs offered by the prison and should make a sincere effort to reestablish and repair family ties. Many people who prepare for release are unrealistic about what they are going to do and lack a workable plan. One example is a person who has no business experience and plans to start a business instead of finding employment. To successfully open a business you must have a business plan and start-up capital, but only about half of all new businesses survive after four years. While your long-term goal may be to start a business, a job may be a more realistic immediate post release objective.

It is also important to remember that companies are required to verify your citizenship before they can hire you. The Immigration and Naturalization Service requires employers to complete a Proof of Identity form (Form I-9) for new hires to prove they are eligible to work in the United States. Review Appendix F and check the list of acceptable documents to ensure you are able to meet this critical pre-employment requirement. After you leave prison is not the time to discover that you do not have a copy of your social security card and birth certificate.

Many employers require that you provide information about the training, skills, and experience that they are looking for. An employment folder that contains your personal information and documents is a good way to do this. The employment folder should include copies of your resume, social security card, birth certificate, high school diploma or General Educational Development certificate, vocational certificates or college diplomas, and a transcript from each school you have attended (include prison schools). Remember to bring extra copies for use during interviews, and to keep the originals with you in your folder.

If you do not have a resume, prepare one and also fill out the sample job application found in this handbook. When you are 60 days or so from release, you should mail resumes and cover letters to employers whose addresses you obtain from the telephone book yellow pages or other sources. You should request an application form in your letter. Plan to follow up with these same employers by telephone or in person and request an interview when you are released. If you do not have access to the yellow pages, you may want to ask a friend, relative, or even your parole officer to send you 10 - 20 addresses from the yellow pages. Remember that employers are looking for people who know what they want to do, who have skills, and who want a career with their company.

Keep in mind that a significant number of ex-offenders have been employed in construction, retail, accommodation, food service, transportation and warehousing jobs. Do not forget to consider employers who hire staff for hotels, colleges, hospitals, and apartment building owners/managers.

If you have access to the Internet, it is a good source for local and national employment information.

Are There Other Employers Who Hire Ex-Offenders

Assume employers will hire you if you are a good match for their needs. One survey of more than 1200 employers report that only eight percent said they would not hire an ex-offender. Since 92 percent of employers will consider hiring you, feel free to look for work from any legitimate source. Limiting yourself to employers that you believe hire ex-offenders can also limit your wages and job prospects. You should try to find employers who are a good match for your skills, experience, and career goals.

Your job search should include all potential employers.

According to Richard Bolles' popular employment book, "What Color Is Your Parachute," some of the best ways to find a job are:

Asking for job-leads from family members, friends, and people in the community has a 33 percent success rate.

Using the phone book's yellow pages to identify subjects or fields of interest to you in the town or city where you will release, and then calling up the employers listed in that field to ask if they are hiring for the type of position you can do and do well, has a 69 percent success rate.

Knocking on the door of any employer, factory, or office that interests you, whether they are known to have a vacancy or not, has a 47 percent success rate.

Remember, the two most critical factors to a successful job search are attitude and persistence. You are marketing a product, yourself, and you have to believe in the product (you) in order to land that job. Also, like any sales situation, you have to market the product (you) and make sure that you make plenty of contacts. Treat your employment search like a job and spend at least 8 hours a day at it. Employers will not usually come looking for you so you have to get out to meet them.

Federal programs are generally designed to help people who need work housing, public assistance, and other services. While each program has different standards for participation with low income being the most common requirement, there are no federal programs exclusively for ex-offenders.

Most assistance programs are administered locally by community agencies. You can find the addresses for them in the local telephone book's blue pages and on the Internet. One of the first stops you should make is to the state employment service office to help you with job leads. Their local addresses are located in the blue pages of the telephone book. You may want to ask the state employment service about job search assistance, federal bonding, employer tax incentives, job training, and Workforce Investment Act - sponsored training. If there are other local agencies or one-stop assistance centers, you may want to contact them as well.

If you are a non-federal offender in a state or local correctional institution, you should ask education services staff for information about community, state, and private programs to help ex-offenders. Assistance may also be available from local faith-based organizations

Your local library may offer public access to the Internet and provide employment information specific to your community. If there is a One-Stop Career Center in your area, be sure to visit it for job leads, training, and other services that can help you and your family. Always explain your situation when you visit any assistance services agencies and, if they cannot be of assistance, do not forget to ask for a referral to another agency or private organization that may be able to help you.

Veterans should contact their local veteran's affairs office for assistance. The VA has a wide range of programs that can be helpful, including rehabilitation services. The Internet website for the VA is www.va.gov, or you can contact their national toll free number at 800-827-1000. Local VA offices are also listed in the government pages of the telephone book. Note: Only veterans with honorable or general discharges are eligible to receive services.

How Do I Get My Birth Certificate?

To obtain a copy of a birth certificate in the United States, write or go to the vital statistics office in the state or area where the event occurred. To ensure that you receive a quick and accurate record upon your request, follow these steps:

Make your letters concise and to the point.

Do not include more than 1 or 2 requests at a time and be careful not to write confusing details of your family history.

Type or print all names and addresses in your letter.

Provide complete information each individual and event for which you need documents.

Include all names, nicknames, and alternate spellings that were used. List dates and types of event as completely and accurately as possible. If you do not know the exact date, specify the span of years you wish searched and be prepared to pay for searches that span several years. Always provide a self addressed stamped envelope.   Internet   address   is: www.usbirthcertificate.net/google/.

Note: The addresses and telephone numbers of the state vital records contact offices are on the following page. You may call or write to them for vital documents. If you write, ask your counselor or case manager for assistance. You should also include a letter from your case manager or counselor indicating who you are or who you claim to be, and the purpose for requesting the record.

State Contacts for Vital Documents	*Some Agencies charge a fee for processing your request*
Alabama Alabama Vital Records P.O. Box 5625 Montgomery AL 36103-5625 334-206-5418	**Arizona** Office of Vital Records Arizona Department of Health Services P.O. Box 3887 Phoenix AZ 85030-3887 602-364-1300/888-816-5907
Alaska Dept of Health Vital Statistics 5441 Commercial Blvd. Juneau AK 99801 907-465-3391	**American Samoa** America Samoa Government Registrar of Vital Records Pago Pago AS 96799 684-633-1406
Arkansas Vital Records POB 8184 Little Rock AR 72203-8184 1-866-209-9482	**Connecticut** Vital Records 410 Capitol Ave MS#11VRS Hartford CT 06106 860-509-7700
California Office of Vital Records Department of Health Services MS5103 P.O. Box 997410 Sacramento CA 95899-7410 916-445-2684	**District of Columbia** Passport Services 1111 19th St NW Suite 510 Washington DC 20522-1705 202-955-0307
Delaware Office of Vital Statistics Division of Public Health 417 Federal Street Dover DE 19903 1-877-888-0248	**Colorado** Vital Records Section 4300 Cherry Creek Drive South HSVRD-VR-A1 Denver CO 80246-1530 303-692-2200
District of Columbia Vital Records Office N Capitol St NE Washington DC 20002 202-671-5500	**Florida** Department of Health Office of Vital Statistics P.O. Box 210 Jacksonville FL 32231 877-550-73306900
Georgia	**Guam**

Department of Human
Resources Vital Records
2600 Skyland Drive NE
Atlanta GA 30319-3640
404-679-4701

Office of Vital Statistics
P.O. Box 2816
Agana, GU, M.I. 96910
671-734-4589

Kansas
Office of Vital Statistics
Curtis State Office Building
1000 SW Jackson
Topeka KS 66612-2221
785-296-1500

Kentucky
Office of Vital Statistics Dept
for Health Services
275 East Main Street
Frankfort KY 40621-0001
502-564-4212

Hawaii
State Department of Health
Vital Statistics Section
P.O. Box 3378
Honolulu HI 96801
808-586-4539

Louisiana
Office of Public Health
Vital Records Registry
POB 60630
New Orleans LA 70160
504-568-5152

Idaho
Bureau of Health Policy
and Vital Statistics
P.O. Box 83720
Boise ID 83720-0036
208-334-5988/1

Maine
Office of Vital Records
Maine Department of H S
244 Water Street
Augusta ME 04333-0011
207-287-3181

Illinois
Division of Vital Records
IL Depart of Public Health
605 W Jefferson St
Springfield IL 62702-5097
217-782-6553

Maryland
Division of Vital Records
6550 Reisterstown Road
P.O. Box 68760
Baltimore MD 21215-0020
410-764-3038

Indiana
Vital Records Dept
State Department of Health
610 Washington
Indianapolis IN 46204
317-233-2700

Massachusetts
Registry of Vital Records
150 Mount Vernon Street
Dorchester MA 02125-3105
617-740-2600

Iowa
Iowa Depart of Public Health
Bureau of Vital Records
321 East 12th Street
Des Moines IA 50319-0075
515-281-4944

Michigan
Vital Records Request
P.O. Box 30721
Lansing MI 48909
517-335-8656

Minnesota
Minnesota Depart of Health
Attn: Office of Registrar
P.O. Box 9441
Minneapolis MN 55440-9441
612-676-5120

Mississippi
Vital Records State
Department of Health
P.O. Box 1700
MS 39215-1700
601-576-7981

Missouri
Missouri Bureau of Vital
Records
P.O. Box 570
Jefferson City MO 65102-0570
573-751-6387

Montana
Office of Vital Statistics
P.O. Box 4210
Helena MT 59604
1-800-877-1946

New Jersey
NJ Vital Statistics
Customer Service Unit
P.O. Box 370
Trenton NJ 08625-0370
609-292-4087

New Mexico
New Mexico Vital Records
P.O. Box 26110
Santa Fe NM 87502
509-841-4185

New York (except New York City)
Certification Unit Vital
Records Section
POB 2602 2nd Floor
800 N Pearl St
Menands, NY 12204
518-474-3075

New York City
Office of Vital Records
NY City Department of Health
125 Worth St/CN4 Room 133
New York, NY 10013-4090
212-788-4520

Nebraska
Vital Records
301 Centennial Mall South
P.O. Box 95065
Lincoln NE 68509-5065
402-471-2871

North Carolina
NC Vital Records
1903 Mail Service Center
Raleigh NC 27699-1903
919-733-3526

Nevada
Office of Vital Records and
Statistics
505 E King Street Room 0102
Carson City NV 89710-4749
775-684-4242

North Dakota
Division of Vital Records
600 East Boulevard Avenue
Dept. 301
Bismarck ND 58505-0200
701-328-2360

New Hampshire
Bureau of Vital Records

Ohio
Vital Statistics

Health and Welfare Building
29 Hazen Drive
Concord NH 03301-6508
603-271-4650

Ohio Department of Health
246 N High Street 1st Floor
Columbus OH 43216
614-466-2585

Oklahoma
Vital Records Service
State Department of Health
1000 Northeast 10th Street
Oklahoma City OK 73117
405-271-4040

Oregon
Oregon Vital Records
P.O. Box 14050
Portland OR 97290-0050
503-731-4000

Rhode Island
Office of Vital Records
3 Capitol Hill Room 101
Providence RI 02908-5097
401-222-2811

Pennsylvania
Division of Vital Records
101 South Mercer Street
P.O. Box 1528
New Castle PA 16101
724-656-3100/

South Carolina
Office of Vital Records SC
DHEC
2600 Bull Street
Columbia SC 29201

Puerto Rico
Dept of Health Demographic
Reg.
P.O. Box 11854
Fernandez Juncos Station
San Juan PR 00910
787-767-9120

South Dakota
Vital Records
State Department of Health
600 East Capitol Avenue
Pierre SD 57501-2536
605-773-4961

Tennessee
Tennessee Vital Records
Central Services Building
421 5th Avenue
North Nashville TN 37247
615-741-1763

Texas
Bureau of Vital Statistics
Texas Department of Health
P.O. Box 12040
Austin TX 78711-2040
888-963-7111

Utah
Office of Vital Records
288 North 1460 West
P.O. Box 141012
Salt Lake City UT 84114
801-538-6105

Vermont
Department of Health
Vital Records Section
P.O. Box 70
108 Cherry Street
Burlington VT 05402

Virginia
Office of Vital Records
P.O. Box 1000
Richmond VA 23218-1000
804-662-6200

Virgin Islands Depart of Health Vital Statistics Charles Harwood Memorial Hosp St. Croix VI 00820 340-774-9000	**West Virginia** Department of Health Vital Registration Office P.O. Box 9709 350 Capitol Charleston WV 25301 360-236-4300
Wisconsin Vital Records Office 1 West Wilson St. P.O. Box 309 Madison WI 53701-0309 608-266-1371	**Wyoming** Vital Records Services Hathaway Building Cheyenne WY 82002 307-777-7591

How Do I Get My Drivers License?

A driver's license is the best form of picture identification and can be a useful in your employment search. Contact the state department of motor vehicles where you will be released for information on how to reinstate or obtain a driver's license. Be sure to include your name, birth date, address, and social security number in your correspondence.

Note: A list of "State Contacts for Driver License Information" is provided on the next page.

Alabama Department of Public Safety Driver's License Division Montgomery, AL 36104 (334) 242-4400	**Alaska** Dept. of Motor Vehicles 2150 E. Dowling Road Anchorage, AK 99507 (907) 269-5551
Arizona Dept of Motor Vehicles P. O. Box 2100 Phoenix, AZ 85001-2100 (602)255-0072 (Phoenix) (800)-252-5866 (Tucson	**Arkansas** Office of Driver Services 7th & Wolfe Street Little Rock, AR 72203 (501) 682-7060
California Dept of Motor Vehicles POB 942890 Sacramento, CA 24290 (800-777-0133	**Colorado** Department of Revenue Motor Vehicle Division 1881 Pierce Street Lakewood, CO 80214 (303) 205-5600
Connecticut Dept of Motor Vehicles 60 State Street Wethersfield, CT 06161 (860) 263-5700	**Delaware** Dept of Motor Vehicles Division of Motor Vehicles P.O. Box 698 Dover, DE 19903 (302) 744-2500
District of Columbia Bureau of Motor Vehicle 301 "C" Street, NW Washington, DC 20001	**Florida** Dept of Motor Vehicles 2900 Apalache Pkwy Tallahassee, FL 32399 (850) 922-9000
Georgia Dept of Driver Services POB 80447 Conyers, GA 30016 (678) 413-8400 (800) 866-754-3687	**Hawaii** Transportation Dept Driver License Section POB 30340 Honolulu, HI 96820-0340 (808) 832-2904
Idaho Transportation Department Driver Services PO Box 7129 Boise, ID 83707-1129 (208) 334-8735	**Illinois** Drivers Services 2701 S. Dirksen Pkwy Springfield, IL 62723 (217) 782-6212

Indiana Bureau of Motor Vehicles 100 North Senate Ave Indianapolis, IN 46204 (317) 233-6000	**Iowa** Office of Driver Services 100 Euclid Avenue Des Moines, IA 50306 (515) 244-9124
Kansas Dept of Motor Vehicles 915 S.W. Harrison Street Topeka, KS 66625 780-296-3963	**Kentucky** Div of Vehicle Licensing 200 Mero Street Frankfort, KY 40652 (502) 564-6800
Louisiana Office of Motor Vehicles P. O. Box 64886 Baton Rouge, LA 70090 (877) 368-5463	**Maine** Bureau of Motor Vehicles State House Station 29 Augusta, ME 04333-0029 (207) 624-9000 (
Maryland Motor Vehicle Admin 6601 Ritchie Hwy NE Glen Burnie, MD 21062 (410) 768-7274	**Michigan** Department of State Driver and Vehicle Records 7064 Crowner Drive Lansing, MI 48918 (888) 767-6424
Minnesota Driver and Vehicle Services 445 Minnesota St, Suite 180 St. Paul, MN 55101 (651) 296-6911	**Mississippi** Driver Services Bureau P. O. Box 958 Jackson, MS 39205 (601) 987-1200
Missouri Drivers License Bureau 301 West High Street Jefferson City, MO 65105 (573) 751-4600	**Montana** Drivers Services Bureau P. O. Box 201430 Helena, MT 59620 (406) 444-3244
Nebraska Dept of Motor Vehicles 301 Centennial Mall South Lincoln, NE 68509 (402) 471-3981	**Nevada** Dept of Motor Vehicles 55 Wright Way Carson City, NV 89711
New Hampshire Division of Motor Vehicles Hazen Drive Concord, NH 03305	**New Jersey** Motor Vehicle Comm. POB 009 Trenton, NJ 08666

(603) 271-2371	609-292-6500
New Mexico Motor Vehicle Division P. O. Box 1028 Santa Fe, NM 87504 1-888-683-4636	**New York State** Dept. of Motor Vehicles 6 Empire State Plaza Albany, NY 12228 (800) 2255368
North Carolina Division of Motor Vehicles 3148 Mail Service Center Raleigh, NC 2769-3101	**North Dakota** Division of Motor Vehicles Driver's License & Traffic Safety 608 East Boulevard Bismark, ND 58505-0700 (701) 328-2600
Ohio Bureau of Motor Vehicles 1970 West Broad Street Columbus, Ohio 43223-1101 (614) 752-7600	**Oklahoma** Department of Public Safety 3600 North ML King Boulevard Oklahoma City, OK 73111 (405) 425-2424
Oregon Driver & Motor Vehicle Ser 1905 Lana Avenue, NE Salem, OR 97314 (503) 945-5000	**Pennsylvania** Driver and Vehicle Services 1101 South Front Street Harrisburg, PA 17104 (717) 412-5300
Rhode Island Division of Motor Vehicles 100 Main Street Pawtucket, RI 02860 401) 588-3020	**South Carolina** Division of Motor Vehicles P. O. Box 1498 Blythewood, SC 29016 (803) 896-5000
South Dakota Dept of Public Safety Drivers Lic 118 West Capitol Avenue Pierre, SD 57501 (605) 773-6883	**Tennessee** Department of Safety Driver License Issuance Div 150 Foster Avenue Nashville, Tennessee 37249
Texas Dept Public Safety POB 4087 Austin, TX 78773-0001 (512) 424-2600	**Vermont** Department of Motor Vehicles 120 State Street Montpelier, Vermont 05603 (802) 828-2000

Virginia Dept Motor Vehicles P. O. Box 27412 Richmond, VA 23269 866-368-5463	**Washington** Dept of Licensing P. O. Box 9030 Olympia, WA 98507-9030 360) 902-3600
West Virginia Dept of Transportation 1800 Kanawha Blvd East Charleston, WV 25317 (304) 558-3900	**Wisconsin** Bureau of Drivers Services 1802 Sheboygan Ave Madison, WI 53707-7918 (608) 266-2353
Wyoming Dept of Transportation Driver Services Division 5300 Bishop Blvd Cheyenne, WY 82009 (307) 777-4800	

Veterans Vocational Rehabilitation and Employment Services

Vocational Rehabilitation and Employment is the VA program that assists veterans with service-connected disabilities to achieve employment or to enhance their ability to function independently at home and in the community.

Benefits include burial, pension, health, home loan, education, life insurance, and vocational rehabilitation. If you are a veteran and want to find out if you are eligible for benefits, contact the VA on their toll-free telephone number at 1-800-827-1000.

For a free pamphlet, Federal Benefits for Veterans and Dependents, contact the Veterans Administration, Office of Public Affairs (80D), 810 Vermont Ave, NW. Washington, DC 20420. To apply for Vocational Rehabilitation and Independent Living Services call the toll-free telephone number, 1-800-827-1000 to request VA Form 28-8832.

Other VA Provided Services and Their Application Procedures:

The VA also provides available vocational and educational guidance and counseling to assist service-members, veterans, and certain dependents of veterans select appropriate career goals and training institutions that use VA educational benefits. Call the nationwide VA toll-free telephone number at 1-800-827-1000 to request VA Form 28-8832, Application for Vocational-Educational Counseling. Internet: www.vba.va.gov/pubs/educationforms.htm for an application for education benefits; or, www.gibill.va.gov/

to access the VA's education web site. If you would like additional information on any of the VA Education programs, please check the Internet: www.vba.va.gov/bln/vre/regional_offices.htm.

How Do I Get Money to Continue My Education?

Federal Student Financial Aid Federal Student Financial Aid consists of Stafford Loans, PLUS Loans, Consolidation Loans, Federal Supplemental Educational Opportunity Grants (FSEOGs), Federal Work-Study, Federal Perkins Loans, and Pell Grants. A Federal Pell Grant, unlike a loan, does not have to be repaid. Generally, Pell Grants are awarded only to undergraduate students who have not earned a bachelor's or professional degree. (A professional degree is usually earned after earning a bachelor's degree in a field such as medicine, law, or dentistry.) For more information, contact: Federal Student Aid Information Center, POB 84, Washington, DC 20044 1-800-433-3243.

-Special Note for those with drug convictions: A law enacted in July 1, 2001 suspends aid eligibility for students convicted under federal or state law of sale or possession of drugs. If you have been convicted for selling drugs, you will be ineligible for two years from the date of your conviction after the first offense, and indefinitely after the second offense. Call 1-800- 433-3243 for more information, or go to www.fafsa.ed.gov, click on "Worksheets" in the left column, then select "Drug Worksheet." Even if you're ineligible for federal aid, you should complete the FAFSA because schools and states use the information in awarding nonfederal aid. You must complete Question 31 of the FAFSA; if you leave it blank, you'll automatically become ineligible for federal student aid.

Loss of Eligibility

If you lose eligibility, you can regain it early by successfully completing an approved drug rehabilitation program. However, a conviction prior to July 1, 2000 could still affect your eligibility if you were convicted for the first time for drug possession on February 1, 2000. You would then be ineligible for SFA program assistance from July 1, 2000 (the implementation date of the law) through January 31, 2001 (one year from the date of the conviction). Instructions on the FAFSA will help you to determine your eligibility under this law.

Remember, just because you were convicted does not automatically mean you still are ineligible for federal aid.

If you are ineligible for federal aid, you should complete the FAFSA because you may be eligible for non-federal aid from states and private institutions. If you regain eligibility during the award year, notify the financial aid administrator at the school that you attend immediately. If you are convicted of a drug-related offense after you submit the FAFSA, you may lose eligibility for federal student aid and you may be liable to return any financial aid received during a period of ineligibility. When you apply for aid from the SFA programs, the U. S. Department of Education verifies some of your information with the following federal agencies: Social Security Administration, Selective Service System, Immigration and Naturalization Service, Department of Justice, and Department of Veterans Affairs.

Special Education Assistance

The National Association of Private Special Education Centers (NAPSEC) is a non-profit association whose mission is to represent private special education programs and affiliated state associations and to ensure access for individuals to appropriate private special education programs and services as vital components of the special education continuum.

You can contact them at: NAPSEC, 1522 K Street, NW, Suite 1032, Washington, DC 20005. Phone: 202-408-3338; Fax: 202-408-3340; Email: napsec@aol.com. Internet: www.napsec.org.

Ex-offenders Voting Rights by States

Convicted felons and ex-offenders typically lose their right to vote in state and federal elections. Almost all states have "disenfranchisement" laws. Only two states, Maine and Vermont, do not place restrictions on an ex-offender's right to vote. Listed below are the number states that place some restrictions on the right to vote for people with felony convictions:

Expungement of Criminal Records. To expunge criminal records is to clear a person's record of a crime committed. A legal professional may assist you to determine how to expunge your record in your state. For more information, check the Internet: www.findcriminal-recordsonline.com.

Job Search Information

Adapted from the U.S. Department of Labor publication, "Tips for Finding the Right Job."

Job Tips for the Ex-offender

Dealing with potential employers is never an easy task for clients with criminal records. Ex-offenders who lie on a job application may get hired, but then fired if their record becomes known. Those who are honest may feel like they never even get a chance. Although there are no magic formulas for dealing with this sensitive situation, the following hints may be helpful. See your release preparation coordinator for more information.

Make a "To Do List" every day and outline daily activities to look for a job.

- Apply for jobs early in the day. This will make a good impression and give you time to complete applications, have interviews, take tests, etc.
- Call employers to find out the best times to apply. Some companies take applications only on certain days and times during the week.
- Write down all employers you contact, the date of your contacts, people you talk to, and special notes about your contacts.
- Apply at several companies in the same area when possible. This saves time and money.
- Be prepared. Have a "master application" and resumes, pens, maps and job information with you all the time. Who knows when a "hot lead" will come your way.
- Follow up leads immediately. If you find out about a job late in the day, call right then! Do not wait until the next day.

Check Points

- Look for job openings with employers who need your job skills.
- Networking. Tell everyone you know you're looking for a job. Ask about openings where your friends work.
- State Employment Service Offices provide help to find jobs and other services, such as career counseling.
- Local public libraries have books on occupations and sometime post local job announcements.
- Community colleges and trade schools sometimes offer counseling and job information to students and the general public.
- Faith-based organizations sometimes offer employment services or provide job search help.
- Government sponsored training programs offer direct placement or short-term training and Government Services.
- Journals and newsletters for professionals or trade associations often advertise job openings in their fields. Ask for these at the public library.

Resume

Be sure to prepare an appropriate resume. You should have enough copies of your resume so that you can leave one with each job interview. If you have several different skills (e.g. short order cook, and heating and air conditioning installer/repairman), you may want to prepare separate resumes.

A resume is a brief summary of your abilities, education, and skills. A resume has one purpose–to get you a job interview. To get someone to interview you, your resume must quickly show that you are worth an interview.

- Gather and check all necessary information. Write down headings such as Education, Experience, Honors, Skills, Activities, and Position. Enter the following information beneath each heading:
- Education can include GED, training certificates, special seminars, summer school, or night school as well as college and university courses. List degrees and month/year obtained, names and locations of schools, and a brief summary of important courses you have taken.
- Experience is full-time paid jobs, academic research projects, internship or co-op positions, part-time jobs, or volunteer work. List the month/years you worked, position, name and location of employer, and your responsibilities at each place.
- Honors is a list of any academic awards (scholarships, fellowships, and honors list), professional awards or recognition, or community awards.
- Skills is a list of computer languages and software, research, laboratory, teaching or tutoring, communication, leadership or athletic, among others.
- Activities is a list of academic, professional, or community organizations in which you hold office or are currently a member. List professional and community activities, including volunteer work. Listing extra-curricular activities or hobbies is optional.
- Position defines the kind of position you want for this job-search. Make notes. Now match your wishes up with positions that are actually available. You can get this information through job postings, ads, personal contacts, or your own research.

- Check for accuracy. You will need full names, full addresses, correct and consistent dates, and correct spellings. Look over what you have written and try to select details of your education, experience, honors, skills, and activities that match an employer's needs in a few more important areas. Organize the resume effectively.
- One final suggestion. You should include a separate cover letter when sending your resume to a prospective employer. The letter should indicate your interest in a particular company or position, summarize the most important parts of your education and experience, and let the employer know where and when you can be contacted for an interview.

Job Applications

If you are asked about felony convictions on an application, consider putting in "will discuss during interview." Since the purpose of an application is to get an interview for the job, putting "will discuss" instead of the possibly damaging information, you are encouraging the employer to either give you the interview to get more information, or eliminate you without really knowing why. If you are a qualified applicant, most employers will want to interview you.

Remember: When you fill out a job application in a company's employment office you should be groomed and dressed as if you were going on an interview. Sometimes you will be interviewed on the spot. When you file an application do not forget about it and hope the employer calls you. Follow-up–usually after 5-7 days. A phone call to check on the status of your application is recommended. In fact, the best advice any job seeker can get is "Do not give up!" There will probably be many "Nos" before you get a job. However, if you're willing to work at getting a job, you will be successful. Good luck!

Possible Phone Scripts for Job Search Situations

FOR CLASSIFIED AD

Hello, my name is _____. I'm calling about the (job title)   position advertised in (name of newspaper   &   edition,   i.e.   Sunday's, yesterday's)_____.

I've had (number of years, or use "a lot" instead of a specific number of years)_____of experience n this field and would like to set up a time for us to get together and discuss this job in more detail.

FOR COLD CALL:

Hello, my name is_____. I'm calling to see if you have any openings for (job your interested in)_____. I've had (number of years, or use "a lot" instead of a specific number of years)_____ of experience in this field and would like to set up a time for us to get together and discuss this job in more detail.

IF THEY DO NOT HAVE OPENINGS

Would it be possible for me to come down and fill out an application in case any positions become available? Do you know of any (job title)_____ openings in the area?

Remember:
Be polite. Whether you get the results you want or not, thank the person for taking the time to speak with you. < Be prepared to answer questions about your background and/or experience. < Have a pen and paper handy to take down information or directions.
Be prepared to set up an interview. This script will give you an idea of how to talk to an employer on the phone. You should always use your own words and use language with which you are comfortable. AVOID SLANG.

Explaining Felony Conviction to Employer

For an ex-offender, the most dreaded part of the job search can be explaining a felony conviction to a potential employer. Many ex-offenders have never honestly answered the question, "Have you ever been convicted of a crime?" on an application. As a result, they drift in and out of employment, staying with a job until the employer finds out through a background check, a call from a parole agent, or some other way.

Ex-offenders may be fired for falsifying information on their job application, not because they are ex-offenders. A company may hire ex-offenders, but have a policy of terminating anyone for lying on the application.

It is up to you whether you tell an employer about felony convictions. But we believe that "honesty is the best policy." Our experience shows that HOW you communicate this information makes a difference. You must see yourself as a worthwhile and valuable asset who has the skills and abilities an employer needs, not as an ex-convict unworthy of employment. You need a positive self-image and confidence in your skills and abilities.

The federal Work Opportunity Tax Credit (WOTC) is available as an incentive to hire ex-offenders and others who may have difficulty in getting work. The Federal Bonding Program, in states where it is available, or the UNICOR Bond Program for federal ex-offenders, allows employers to hire ex-felons and bond them. These incentives, along with your positive attitude and qualifications, can make you an attractive job candidate.

Sample Resume

Example: Simple Chronological Resume
Your Name
Street Address
Your Town, IN 47000
Phone: (000) 000-0101
FAX: (000) 000-1100
E-mail: yourname@online.com

Job Objective
This is a very brief statement on "the type of work" you are seeking. This is the first place an employer looks on any resume. It tells the employer your purpose in finding a job.

Highlights of Qualifications
List the main qualities that make you qualified for the job, including character traits, chief skills and strengths. Include significant commendations, awards, and honors you have received for previous jobs.

Relevant skills and experience
List all dates of employment by the most recent job first
Name(s) of employers and organizations
Title(s) of the positions you held
Brief description of your job responsibilities for each past position

Education

References

Provide past job references as requested

Chronological Resume (Example)

Name
Address
Telephone Number(s) (Day); Evening
Job Objective:
   Match with qualifications, employment, and
   education

Highlights of Qualifications
Number of years experience
Quick learner
Dependable, timely worker
Easy personality and works well with others

Employment History
   From (Month/Year) to Present (List all past
   employers in this format) Name and Address of
   Employer: Title:

Prepare (use action words to describe duties)
Demonstrate
Manage

Education
   List School(s) and locations Graduated?
   Diploma? Degree?

References
Available upon request of employer

Sample Job Application

The following sample job application will give you an idea of what to expect when you apply for a job. You may be asked to fill out an application on the day of the interview, so make sure you are prepared to provide any necessary information about yourself and your employment history.

Retail   Systems   Corporation--Application   for Employment

Personal Information

First Name: _____

Middle Name: _____

Last Name: _____

Social Security Number: _____

Street Address: _____

City: _____ State: _____ Zip: ___

Home Phone: _____

Business Phone: _____

Have you ever applied for employment with us?
Yes: _____ No: _____ If yes, when?:_____

Position Desired

Title: _____

Desired Salary: $_____

If you prefer to work in a different zip code than where you currently live, please indicate where you would like to be located below.

City: _____ State: _____ Zip: _____

Work Eligibility Are you eligible to work in the United States? Yes: _____ No: _____

Are you available to work holidays? Yes: _____ No: _____ When will you be available to begin work? _____/_____ (Month/Year) Are you 17 or older? Yes: _____ No: _____ Have you been convicted of or pleaded no contest to a felony within the last five years? Yes: _____ No: _____ If yes, please explain:

Have you been convicted of, pleaded guilty to, or pleaded no contest to, an act of dishonesty, or breach of trust or moral turpitude, such as misdemeanor petty theft, burglary, fraud, writing bad checks, and other related crimes within the last five (5) years? * Yes: _____ No: _____ If yes, please explain: _____

Do you have other special training or skills (additional spoken or written languages, computer software knowledge, machine operation experience, etc.)?

How did you hear of our organization?

*Conviction of a crime, or pleading guilty to a criminal charge, will not necessarily disqualify you from the job for which you are applying. Each conviction or plea will be considered with respect to time, job relatedness, and other relevant factors.

Availability

Days Available: Sun. ____ Mon. ____ Tues. ____ Wed. ____ Th.____ Fri. ____ Sat. ____

Total Hours Available: ___ Hours Available: from ___ to____

Education

High School: _____

City: _____ State: _____

College:_____

City:_____ State: _____

Course of Study: _____

# of Years Completed: _____

Did You Graduate? Yes: _____ No: _____

Degree: _____

Employment History

Please give accurate and complete full-time employment record. Start with present or most recent employer. Include military experience applicable.

Position #1

Company Name: _____

City: _____ State: _____

Company Phone Number: _____

Job Title: _____

Name of Supervisor: _____

Employed (Month and Year) From: _____ To: _____

Weekly Pay: _____

Describe your work: _____

May we contact this employer? Yes: _____ No:

_____

If not, why not? _____

Reason for leaving: _____

Position #2

Company Name: _____

City: _____ State: _____

Company Phone Number: _____

Job Title: _____

Employed (Month and Year) From: _____ To: _____

Weekly   Pay: _____   Describe   your   work:

_____

May we contact this employer? Yes: _____ No: _____

If not, why not? _____

Reason for leaving: ____

Position #3

Company Name: _____

City:_____ State: _____

Company Phone Number: _____

Job Title: _____

Name of Supervisor: _____

Employed (Month and Year) From: _____ To:

Weekly Pay: _____

Describe your work: _____

May we contact this employer? Yes: _____ No: _____

If not, why not? _____

Reason for leaving: _____

Appendix B

Answering Your Questions

The following Frequently asked questions and answers about parole are from the U.S. Department of Justice Parole Commission website (http://www.usdoj.gov: 80/index.html), and pertain to Federal prisoners (anyone committed of a Federal offenses and served time in Federal prison). Individual states have their own versions of conditions and requirements for parole or conditional release, however, they do not differ that much. Use the contact information in Appendix "A" or "B" of this book to request parole information specific to where you live or intend to live.

What is Parole?

When someone is paroled, they serve part of their sentence under the supervision of their community. The law says that the U.S. Parole Commission may grant parole if (a) the inmate has substantially observed the rules of the institution; (b) release would not depreciate the seriousness of the offense or promote disrespect for the law; and (c) release would not jeopardize the public welfare. Parole has a three-fold purpose: (1) through the assistance of the United States Probation Officer, a parolee may obtain help with problems concerning employment, residence, finances, or other personal problems which often trouble a person trying to adjust to life upon release from prison; (2) parole protects society because it helps former prisoners get established in the community and thus prevents many situations in which they might commit a new offense; and (3) parole prevents needless imprisonment of those who are not likely to commit further crime and who meet the criteria for parole. While in the community, supervision will be oriented toward reintegrating the offender as a productive member of society.

How does the Commission determine if someone is eligible for Parole?

A criminal offender becomes eligible for parole according to the type of sentence received from the court. The "parole eligibility date" is the earliest time the offender might be paroled. If the Parole Commission decides to grant parole, it will set the date of release, but the date must be on or after the "eligibility" date.

The process begins at sentencing. Unless the court has specified a minimum time for the offender to serve, or has imposed an "indeterminate" type of sentence, parole eligibility occurs upon completion of one-third of the term. If an offender is serving a life sentence or a term or terms of 30 years or more he or she will become eligible for parole after 10 years.

How does one apply for parole?

To apply for parole, the offender has to fill out and sign an application furnished by a case manager. Everyone except those committed under juvenile delinquency procedures who wish to be considered for parole must complete a parole application.

In some instances, the offender may not wish to apply for parole – if this is the case the offender is provided a waiver as opposed to an application.

How is one notified of hearings?

A case manager notifies the offender when his or her parole hearing is scheduled. The initial hearing will usually take place within a few months after arrival at the institution. The only exception to this rule is if the offender is serving a minimum term of ten years or more, in which case the initial hearing will be scheduled six month before the completion of ten years.

What happens at a parole hearing?

A parole hearing is an opportunity for the offender to present his or her side of the story, and express their own thoughts as to why they feel they should be paroled. Many subjects come up during the course of the hearing. These typically include the details of the offense, prior criminal history, the guidelines which the Commission uses in making their determination, the offender's accomplishments in the correctional facility, details of a release plan, and any problems the offender has had to meet in the past and is likely to face again in the future.

The Commission is interested in both the public safety as well as the needs of the individual.

When is a decision made about parole?

A Parole Examiner reviews the case file before the hearing occurs. A recommendation relative to parole is made at the conclusion of the hearing and in most instances, the offender is notified of that recommendation. If a recommendation is not provided, the Examiner may refer the case to the Commission's Office for further review. All recommendations made at the hearing are only tentative as another examiner review is required before a final decision is made. Usually it takes about 21 days for the offender to receive a Notice of Action advising them of the official decision.

Is it possible to appeal the parole decision?

Certainly. Within 30 days of the date on the Notice of Action, the offender may file an appeal with the National Appeals Board. Case Managers will have a copy of the form used for appeal. After receiving the appeal, the National Appeals Board may affirm, reverse or modify the Commission's decision, or may order a new hearing. A decision by the National Appeals Board is final.

Decisions made under the District of Columbia are not eligible for the administrative appeal process. These prisoners must appeal through D.C. Superior Court.

What kind of job can a parolee get?

In most cases, any legitimate employment is normally acceptable. Full time work is preferable to part time work; work done continuously at one location is generally better than work in which it is necessary to travel. It is expected that the job will provide enough income to support dependents. In some cases, the Parole Commission may prohibit certain types of employment. If, for example, the original offense behavior involved abuse of a certain occupational position and there might be a likelihood of further criminal conduct if returned to such employment, than that employment may be denied.

What does a parolee do if he or she has no home to go to?

The U.S. Parole Commission is interested in parolees having a suitable place to live. Sometimes this is with family or relatives, but in other cases, the Commission may consider an independent living agreement more suitable to the parolees – and the community's – needs. There is no rigid rule that requires parolees to reside in their home, if they have one, or that they cannot be paroled if they do not.

If I have more questions, whom do I ask?

You may contact the U.S. Parole Commission by writing us at 5550 Friendship Boulevard, Suite 420

Chevy Chase, MD 20815-7286. We would like to help you answer any further questions you may have

Is parole the same as probation?

No. Probation is a period of supervision in the community imposed by the court as an alternative to imprisonment. Parole is the release of a prisoner to supervision in the community after he/she has completed a part of his/her sentence in an institution.

Can an offender be allowed to see his or her file before the hearing?

The Notice of Hearing form will tell the offender that he or she may review their institutional file before the hearing. Law from being shown exempts certain parts of the file. Such exempted parts will be summarized, however, and the summary furnished to the offender if asked. If the offender asks to see his or her file, or part of it, he or she may inspect any documents, except the exempted ones, which the Parole Commission uses as a basis for its decision about parole. The Case Manager can explain what types of material are exempted by law, and can assist in requesting files for review. He/she can also discuss the possibility of reviewing the offender's file at some time other than just before the parole hearing.

May the offender bring someone into the hearing room?

The Notice of Hearing form provides a place for the offender to name someone as his or her representative at the hearing. The representative should be given timely prior notice by the offender to allow adequate time to prepare for the hearing. This representative would, with the final approval of the examiner conducting the hearing, ordinarily be allowed to enter the hearing room and make a brief statement on the offender's behalf. The offender may elect to waive representation by initialing the appropriate section on the Notice of Hearing form. Permission must be granted from this individual, and he or she must be given enough time to plan to attend the hearing. The representative may enter the hearing room with the offender and make a brief statement on his or her behalf. Should the offender decide not to have a representative, he or she will be asked to initial the waiver section on the Notice of Hearing form.

Who else will be present at the parole hearing?

Generally, a Hearing Examiner from the Parole Commission will conduct the hearing. The Case Manager generally also will attend the hearing. Observers may ask to come into the hearing room occasionally. These are usually members of the institution staff or personnel of the Parole Commission. A person who wishes to speak in opposition to an offender's parole may also appear at the hearing.

Are the hearings recorded?

Yes, the interview is recorded. The offender may request a copy of the recording by submitting a request under the Freedom of Information Act.

Does the judge or other court official make a recommendation to the Commission regarding parole?

The Judge who sentenced the criminal offender, the Assistant United States Attorney who prosecuted the case and the defense attorney may make recommendations regarding parole. These recommendations are generally submitted to the

Commission before the first hearing and become a part of the material the Commission considers. The Judge's recommendation and the defense attorney's recommendation will be made on Form AO-235. The Assistant United States Attorney's recommendation will be on Form USA-792.

Does the Hearing Examiner usually follow the recommendations made by the institution staff?

Institution staff recommendations if provided are given thoughtful consideration but are not always followed, as they are only one of the several factors considered by the Examiner and the Commission.

How do any of the following situations affect parole?

Institution misconduct. The prisoner is expected to observe the rules of the institution in which confined to be eligible for parole. Misconduct resulting in forfeited or withheld good time indicates that institution rules have not been observed and is a poor argument for parole, but does not automatically disqualify the applicant from Commission consideration.

Presence of a detainer. A detainer does not of itself constitute a basis to deny parole. A prisoner may be paroled to a detainer indicating an actual release to the custody of another jurisdiction. If the detainer is dropped, the parole will occur, with an approved plan, directly to the community. In some circumstances, parole may be to the detainer only and if the detainer is dropped, further action regarding parole will not occur, pending additional review by the Commission.

Alien subject to deportation. In some cases, the Commission grants parole on condition that the alien be deported and remain outside the United States. In other cases, the Commission merely grants parole to an immigration detainer. In such instances, the individual does not leave the institution until the immigration officials are ready to receive him.

Case in court on appeal. All persons have the right by law to appeal their conviction and sentence. The Parole Commission recognizes this right and the existence of a court appeal has no bearing whatever on parole decisions.

Will parole be granted if there is an unpaid committed fine?

A fine for which an offender is to "stand committed" must be taken care of in some way before the Commission can take action on the "time portion" of the sentence. The usual way to take care of a fine is to pay it. If an offender cannot do so, he or she may apply to take an "indigent prisoner's oath" if the offender can show that there are no funds or assets in his or her possession. A Case Manager can help the offender apply to take this oath. If the offender can neither pay the fine nor qualify for the oath, the Warden or Magistrate might determine that the offender needs all of his or her money or assets to support dependents. In some cases, the offender may be able to pay part of the fine and the Warden or Magistrate will determine that he or she needs the remainder of the assets for the support of dependents. In such cases, however, the offender still has a civil requirement to pay the fine at some later date.

If the offender has sufficient money or assets to pay the committed fine but fails to do so, the offender will not be paroled.

Are reasons provided if parole is not granted?

Yes, the Hearing Examiner will discuss the recommendation with the offender at the time of the hearing, and the Notice of Action will state the reasons for the decision.

If parole is not granted at the initial hearing, will the offender be given another hearing?

By law, if a sentence is less than seven years the offender will be granted another hearing after 18 months from the time of his or her last hearing. If the sentence is seven years or more the next hearing is scheduled 24 months from the time of the last hearing. The first Statutory Interim Hearing may be delayed until the docket preceding eligibility if there is more than 18 or 24 months between the initial hearing and the eligibility date.

If the Commission does not parole the offender earlier, can he or she be paroled later on near the end of the term?

If the sentence is five years or longer, the law provides that the offender will be granted mandatory parole by the Commission when he or she has served two-thirds of the term or terms, unless the Commission makes a finding either that (1) the offender has seriously or frequently violated institution rules and regulations, or (2) there is a reasonable probability that the offender will commit a further crime. If an offender is serving a life term or consecutive terms, a Case Manager can explain the law in relation to parole at the two-thirds point.

Will an offender be given a hearing just before the "two-thirds" date?

If an offender is serving a sentence of five years or larger, the case will be reviewed on the record shortly before the "two-thirds" date arrives. If the offender is not granted mandatory parole based on a "record review", he or she will be scheduled for a hearing when the Hearing Examiner next visits the institution. A decision about parole will then follow that hearing.

May an offender waive parole at the two-thirds point of the sentence?

Yes. If the offender chooses to waive parole at this point, release will occur at the mandatory release date of the sentence.

If someone is paroled after two-thirds of a sentence, must they comply with the parole conditions like any other parolee?

Yes. A parolee must abide by the conditions of release, and parole may be revoked if any of them are violated. Parolees will remain under supervision until the expiration of his or her sentence unless the Commission terminates supervision earlier. The reduction of supervision time by 180 days provided by the mandatory release laws does not apply to this type of parole.

If parole is not granted to an offender at any time during his or her sentence, when does he or she get out?

Unless the offender has a forfeited all statutory good time, he or she will be released via Mandatory Release. The Mandatory Release date is computed by the institution officials according to how much statutory good time the offender is entitled to and how much "extra" good time is earned. The law states that a mandatory release "shall upon release be treated as if released on parole and shall be subject to all provisions of the law relating to the parole of United States prisoners until the expiration of the maximum term or terms for which he was sentenced, less 180 days." This means a parolee should have a release plan as if he or she were going out on parole. The release will be supervised by a United States Probation Officer as if on parolee until 180 days before the expiration date of the sentence provided the releasee does not violate the conditions of release, in which case the Commission retains jurisdiction to the original full term date of the sentence.

If an offender is not paroled and has less than 180 days left on a sentence when they are released, they will be released without supervision. However, if a special parole term is being served, supervision will terminate at the full term date. The 180-day date does not apply.

If the Parole Commission grants parole, when will a parolee be released?

If a parolee's parole plan is complete and has been approved by the Parole Commission following an investigation by the United States Probation Officer, release will be on the date set by the Commission (assuming, of course, that the parole is not retarded or rescinded for misconduct or for some other reason). If the plan is not approved, release may be delayed regardless of the effective date which the Commission set when it granted parole.

What type of release plan must be in order?

A release plan should normally include a suitable residence and a verified offer of employment. A parole advisor is necessary only if the Commission or the United States Probation Officer specifically says that one should be obtained. There are exceptions. For example, a definite job is sometimes neither necessary nor possible. The Commission always considers the individual's situation and may waive this or any other standard requirement if it sees fit to do so. On the other hand, special requirements may be added and must be met before release.

How can a parolee get a job while still in the institution?

Relatives, friends, and social agencies in the community where a parolee wishes to live or former employers are likely contacts. If a parolee is released through a Community Corrections Center this is also a time during which he or she may find employment.

The United States Probation Officer to whom the parolee reports investigates job offers, and that officer reports back to the institution and the Parole Commission.

Must a parolee return to the community from which he or she came?

In most instances, a parolee will be released to the Judicial District in which he or she was convicted or the Judicial District of legal residence. The parolee's former community may offer the best opportunity for the help and support that will be needed. If the Commission believes, however, that the chance of success on parole is greater in another community, it may order residence in a different Judicial District.

After a parolee is released, to whom and when does the parole report?

Unless a parolee is released to a detainer, he or she will go to an approved residence and report within three days to the United States Probation Office shown on the release certificate. The parolee will continue to report to a Probation Officer in person as instructed by the officer. In addition, monthly written reports are required as long as parolees remain under supervision on your sentence.

Upon what conditions is a parolee released on parole or mandatory release?

The conditions are indicated on the release certificate presented to the parolee when he or she is released or on the Notice of Action.

If the prisoner is denied parole, he or she will be released at a date provided by deducting the sum total of good time days from the full term date. The conditions of supervision will be specified on the certificate of mandatory release.

May any of the conditions of release be changed by the Commission?

If a parolee believes the conditions on the Certificate of Release are unfair, he or she may ask the Case Manager for an appeal form and submit it to the Regional Commissioner within 30 days after release. The Commission will consider the appeal and the parolee will be notified of the decision. While the appeal is pending, the parolee must continue to abide by the conditions imposed.

After a parolee is released, may any of the conditions be changed? Can additional ones be imposed?

The Probation Officer or the Commission itself may propose changing or adding to the conditions. The parolee will be notified of any such proposal and will be allowed up to ten days to make any written comments to the Commission. A form for this purpose is made available to the parolee, and it can be used for comments. The parolee may write directly to the Commission (with a copy to his or her Probation Officer) if he or she wishes to have any of the conditions amended or deleted.

May a parolee be required to go into a halfway house or undergo some course of treatment for drug or alcohol use while under supervision?

Federal law permits the Commission to require a parolee to participate in any of the programs mentioned for all or part of the time under supervision. In most cases, a parolee will be notified in advance and may submit comments about the proposal to the Commission before the final decision is made.

May a parolee own, use or possess firearms after they are released?

Except in very rare situations, federal law forbids anyone who has ever been convicted of a felony from possessing firearms or ammunition. Generally, therefore, parolees will not be permitted to own or possess a firearm or ammunition.

How long will a parolee remain under supervision after his or her release?

Parolees will remain under the jurisdiction of the Parole Commission and under supervision of a Probation Officer until the maximum expiration date of the sentence, unless the Commission terminates supervision earlier. If the parolee's supervision is terminated early, he or she will be given a Certificate of Early Termination.

If an offender is not paroled, but instead mandatorily released, supervision automatically ends 180 days before the maximum expiration date, unless the Commission terminates supervision earlier and issues a Certificate of Early Termination.

How does the Commission decide whether to terminate supervision early?

A Probation Officer will submit an annual report to the Commission about a parolee's adjustment in the community. After reviewing the report including any recommendations, the Commission may decide to terminate parolee supervision early. By law, the Commission must consider a case after the second year in the community (not counting any time spent in confinement since release), and every year thereafter.

After five years of supervision in the community the Commission must terminate a parolee's supervision unless it finds that there is a likelihood that you will engage in conduct violating any law. Any finding of that nature will be made only after the parolee has had an opportunity for a personal hearing. A parolee may choose to waive the hearing if so desired.

What happens if a parolee violates the conditions of parole or mandatory release?

A Probation Officer reports the violation to the Parole Commission and a Commissioner determines the appropriate sanctions, including the possibility of issuance of an arrest warrant or a summons for the parolee to appear at a hearing. The Probation Officer is required to report any and all violations, but may recommend that the parolee be continued under supervision. The Probation Officer's recommendation is one of the factors considered by the Commission in its decision.

Who issues a warrant or summons if a parolee violates parole or mandatory release?

Only a Parole Commissioner may issue a warrant or a summons for a violation of the conditions of release.

After a warrant or summons is issued, what happens then?

The parolee is either taken into custody or summoned to appear at a hearing. Custody is usually in the nearest government approved jail or detention center. Unless the offender has been convicted of a new offense, a Probation Officer will personally advise the offender of his or her legal rights and conduct a preliminary interview. The Probation Officer will discuss the charges that have been placed against the offender and then submit a report to the Commission. In this report, the Probation Officer will recommend whether there is "probable cause" to believe that a violation has occurred and whether the offender should be held in custody pending a revocation hearing or be reinstated to supervision. The Probation Officer will advise the offender of the recommendation and the basis for it.

After the Probation Officer's report is received, the Regional Commissioner will either order the parolee reinstated to supervision or order him or her held for a revocation hearing by a Hearing Examiner.

If a parolee is convicted of a new offense, they are not entitled to a preliminary interview because the conviction is sufficient evidence that they did violate the conditions of release. In such case, the offender may be transported without delay to a federal institution for a revocation hearing.

May a parolee have an attorney at a preliminary interview and revocation hearing?

Yes, parolees are entitled to an attorney of their choice (or have one appointed by the court if one cannot be afforded). It is the responsibility of the parolee to keep his or her attorney advised as to the time and place of the hearing.

Where are the revocation hearings held?

Generally, revocation hearings are held after the offender is returned to a federal institution. Such institutional hearings are held within 90 days from the time the offender was taken into custody based on the Commission's warrant.

If there are sufficient reasons to do so, the Commission may order a parolee's revocation hearing held in his or her own community or in the community where he or she was arrested. The offender will be entitled to such a hearing only if the offender denies violating the conditions of release, and if the offender was not convicted of a new crime. If a local revocation hearing is requested, the parolee must complete a form. There is a penalty for false answers on this form, and a denial of violation must be honestly made. Local revocation hearings are generally held within 60 days from the date the Regional Commissioner finds "probable cause" that parole or mandatory release was violated.

If the offender's hearing is held in a Federal Institution rather than locally, may he or she also have an attorney and witnesses?

The offender is not entitled to appointed counsel, but may secure an attorney at his own expense. The attorney can act only in the capacity of a representative.

If the Commission revokes parole or mandatory release, does a parolee get any credit on the sentence for the time spent under supervision?

Generally, if an offender is convicted of a new law violation, he or she is not entitled to credit for any of the time spent under supervision unless serving a YCA or NARA commitment. Also, there is no credit given for any time a parolee intentionally failed to respond or report to a Probation Officer or after a parolee has absconded from his or her area and the Probation Officer did not know where he or she was living. For violation of any of the other noncriminal conditions, a parolee generally will be credited for all of the time spent under supervision in the community.

If a parolee is revoked rather than reinstated to supervision, or if he or she is not re-paroled *immediately, how long must I serve before the Commission reviews my case again?*

The Commission utilizes its guidelines to help in determining the length of time a parolee should serve. The guidelines are the same ones used for inmates who apply for their initial parole hearings. Decisions, of course, can be made above or below the guidelines for good cause.

Appendix C

Federal & Military Parole/Probation Agencies

The U.S. Parole Commission is an independent agency within the Department of Justice that has jurisdiction over all decisions to grant, deny, or revoke parole for Federal Offenders, (anyone convicted of a United States or Federal Code Offense).

U.S. Parole Commission
5550 Friendship Boulevard
Suite 420
Chevy Chase, MD 20815-7286
Ph: 1-301-492-5990 Fax: 1-301-442-6699

All offenders whom the U.S. Parole Commission has released on probation, parole, or conditional release are supervised by U.S. probation officers with offices in Federal District Courts throughout the United States.

1st Circuit Court 1 Courthouse Way Suite 2500 Boston, MA 02210 (617) 748-9057	Maine, Rhode Island Massachusetts, New Hampshire, Puerto Rico
2nd Circuit Court U.S. Courthouse 40 Foley Square Clerks Office; Rm 1702 New York, NY 10007 (212) 857-8700	Connecticut, New York, Vermont
3rd Circuit Court United States Courthouse 601 Market Streets Philadelphia, PA 19106 (215) 597-2995	Pennsylvania, West New York
4th Circuit Court 501 U.S. Courthouse Annex 1100 East Main Street Richmond, VA 23219	Maryland, North Carolina, South Carolina, Virginia, and West Virginia

(804) 916-2700	
5th Circuit Court 600 Camp Street New Orleans, LA 70130 (504) 589-6514	Louisiana, Mississippi, Texas
6th Circuit Court Potter Stewart U.S. Courthouse 100 E. Fifth Street Cincinnati, Ohio 45202-3988 (513) 564-7000	Kentucky, Michigan, Ohio, Tennessee
7th Circuit Court 219 S. Dearborn Street Chicago, IL 60604 (312) 435-5850	Illinois, Indiana, Wisconsin
8th Circuit Court Thomas F. Eagleton Court House 111 S. 10TH St. St. Louis, M 63102 (314) 244-2400.	Arkansas, Iowa, Minnesota, Missouri, Nebraska, North Dakota, South Dakota
9th Circuit Court Post Office Box 193939 San Francisco, CA 94119-3939 (415) 556-9800	Alaska, Arizona, California, Hawaii, Idaho, Montana, Nevada, Northern Mariana Island, Oregon, Washington
10th Circuit Court Byron White U.S. Courthouse 1823 Stout Street Denver, CO 80257 303-844-3157	Colorado, Kansas, New Mexico, Oklahoma, Utah, Wyoming
11th Circuit Court E. P. Tuttle Court Building 56 Forsyth Street N.W. Atlanta, GA 30303 (404) 335-6100	Alabama, Florida, Georgia
U.S. Air Force Clemency and Parole Board	1535 Command Drive EE Wing, 3rd Floor Andrews AFB, Maryland 20762-7002
U.S. Army Clemency and Parole Board	1941 Jefferson Davis Hway CCM4 Arlington, VA 22202 703-607-1504
U.S. Naval Clemency and Parole Board	901 M. St, SE, Bldg. 36 Randolph Street Washington, DC 20374 202-685-6457

Appendix D

State Parole Offices

Each state controls it's own prison and parole system and the rules and structure vary. Some states have abolished their parole systems and prisoners must serve their entire sentence, or the majority of their sentence, before being released. In some states the prisons, the parole boards/commission, and the supervising parole officers are from separate departments within the state. For instance, in New Jersey the Department of Corrections (DOC) (who rules the prisons), and the Parole Board (who decides who is/is not granted parole, who is denied parole, and whose parole is revoked. New Jersey parole officers are from the Bureau of Parole, which is under the DOC.

Few, if any, states release prisoners back into society without some degree of supervision. The following are contacts where anyone can get information and answers to questions.

Alabama Board of Parole and Pardons ☺	50 North Ripley Street Gordon Parsons Building Montgomery, Alabama 36130 334-242-8700
Alaska Board of Parole ☺	P.O. Box 112000 2000 907-465-3384
Arizona Board of Executive Clemency ☻	1645 W. Jefferson, Suite 326 Phoenix, Arizona 85007 606-542-5656
Arizona Board of Executive Clemency	P.O. Box 34085 Little Rock, Arkansas 72203 501-682-3850
California Board of Prison Terms	428 J Street, Sixth Floor Sacramento, California 916-324-0557
Colorado Board of Parole	1600 W. 24th Street

	Pueblo, Colorado 719-583-5800
Connecticut Board of Parole	21 Grand Street Hartford, Connecticut 06116 860-692-7402
Delaware Board of Parole	Carvel State Building 820 North French Street Wilmington, Delaware 302-577-5233
Florida Parole Commission	2601 Blairstone Road Tallahassee, Florida 850-487-1980
Georgia Board of Pardons and Parole	2 Martin Luther King Drive Fifth Floor, East Tower Atlanta, Georgia 30334 404-651-6667
Hawaii Paroling Authority	1177 Alakea Street Honolulu, Hawaii 96813 808-587-1310
Idaho Commission for Pardons and Parole	3125 S. Shoshone Street Boise, Idaho 83705 208-334-2520
Illinois Prisoner Review Board	319 E. Madison Springfield, Illinois 62701 217-782-7273
Indiana Parole Board	302 W. Washington Indianapolis, Indiana 46204 317-232-5737
Iowa Board of Parole	420 Keo Way (Holmer-Murphy Bldg.) Des Moines, Iowa 50309 515-242-5749
Kansas Parole Board **Landon State Office Building**	900 S.W. Jackson Topeka, Kansas 66612 785-296-3469
Kentucky Parole Board	500 State Office Building Frankfort, Kentucky 40601 502-564-3620
Louisiana Board of Parole	P.O. Box 94304, Capital Station Baton Rouge, LA 79804 504-342-6622
Maine Parole Board	State House Station 111 Augusta, Maine 04333 207-287-2711
Maryland Parole Commission	Plaza Office Center, Suite 307 6776 Reistertown Road Baltimore, Maryland 21215

	410-585-3210
Massachusetts Parole Board	27-43 Wormwood Street Boston, Massachusetts 02210 617-727-3271
Michigan Parole Board	Grandview Plaza Building P.O. Box 30003 Lansing, Michigan 48909 517-373-0270
Minnesota Office of Adult Release	1450 Energy Park Drive St. Paul, Minnesota 55108 651-642-0270
Mississippi Parole Board	201 W. Capitol Street Jackson, Mississippi 39201 601-354-7716
Missouri Board of Probation and Parole	1511 Christy Drive Jefferson City, Missouri 65101 573-526-6550
Nebraska Board of Parole	P.O. Box 94754 State House Station Lincoln, Nebraska 68509 402-471-2156
Nevada Board of Parole Commissioners	1445 Hot Springs Road Carson City, Nevada 89711 775-687-5049
New Hampshire Adult Parole Authority	New Hampshire State Prison P.O. Box 14 Concord, New Hampshire 03301 603-271-2569
New Jersey State Parole Board	P.O. Box 862, Whittelsey Road Trenton, New Jersey 08625 609-984-6263
New Mexico Adult Parole Board	4351 State Road 14 Santa Fe, New Mexico 87505 505-827-8825
New York Board of Parole	97 Central Avenue Albany, New York 12206 518-473-9548
North Carolina Post-Release and Parole Commission	P.O. Box 29540 2020 Yonge Road Raleigh, North Carolina 27626
North Dakota Parole Board	P.O. Box 370 Dickinson, ND 58602 701-328-6190
Ohio Parole Board	1050 Freeway Drive North Columbus, Ohio 43229 614-752-1200
Oklahoma Board of Parole	4040 N. Lincoln, Suite 219

	Oklahoma City, Oklahoma 73105 405-427-8601
Oregon Board of Parole and Post Prison Supervision	2575 Center Street, N.E. Salem, Oregon 97310 503-945-0904
Pennsylvania Board of Probation and Parole	1101 S. Front Street Harrisburg, PA 17104 717-787-5100
Rhode Island Parole Board	1 Center Place Providence, RI 02903 401-222-3262
South Carolina Board of Probation, Parole and Pardon Services	P.O. Box 50666 Columbia, SC 29250 803-734-9278
South Dakota Board of Pardons and Parole	P.O. Box 911 Sioux Falls, South Dakota 57117 605-339-6780
Tennessee Board of Paroles	404 James Robertson Parkway Nashville, Tennessee 37219 615-741-1673
Texas	Price Daniel Building 209 West 14th Austin, Texas 78701 512-475-3407
Utah Board of Pardons and Parole	448 East, 6400 South, #300 Murray, Utah 84107 801-261-6464
Vermont Board of Parole	103 South Main Street Waterbury, Vermont 05676 802-241-2294
Virginia Parole Board	6900 Atmore Drive Richmond, Virginia 23225 804-674-3081
Washington Intermediate Sentence Review Board	4713 Sixth Avenue, S.E. Olympia, WA 98504 360-493-9271
Wisconsin Parole Commission	P.O. Box 7925 Madison, Wisconsin 53707 608-267-0921
Wyoming Board of Parole	1614 Gannett Drive Riverton, Wyoming 82501 307-857-5110
District of Columbia (U.S. Parole Commission)	5550 Friendship Blvd Chevy Chase, MD 20815 301-492-5990

American Probation and Parole Association	2760 Research Park Drive Lexington, KY 40511Phone: (859) 244-8203
Guam Territorial Parole Board	P.O. Box 3236 Agana, Guam 96910 671-473-7001
Puerto Rico Board of Parole	P.O. Box 40945, Minillas Station San Juan, Puerto Rico 00940 787-754-8115
Virgin Islands Board of Parole	P.O. Box 2668 St. Thomas, U.S. Virgin Islands 00801 809-774-0270
Canada National Parole Board 410 Laurier Avenue West Ottawa, Ontario, Canada K1A OR1	613-954-6120 or 410 Laurier Ave. W. Ottawa, Ontario KIAORI (613) 954-6120

Breinigsville, PA USA
31 August 2009
223266BV00001B/1/P